god
struck
me
dead

Religious Conversion Experiences and
Autobiographies of Ex-slaves

Clifton H. Johnson, Editor
Foreword by Paul Radin

Pilgrim Press

Philadelphia   Boston

Copyright © 1969
United Church Press
Philadelphia, Pennsylvania
Library of Congress Catalog Card No. 78–77839

Preface

Scholars who are today engaged in reinterpreting and reevaluating American history in terms of the contributions of minority groups recognize a heavy indebtedness to Charles S. Johnson, Paul Radin, and other members of the Fisk University Social Science Institute for their pioneer research in the field of Negro life and culture. Under Dr. Johnson's direction, the Institute, in the 1930's, became one of the leading research centers for the social sciences in the nation. While pioneering in research methods and areas of study, the Institute was also preserving for future scholars documentary evidence of the contemporary scene: of the South in general and of the Negro in particular.

Between 1928 and 1940, the Social Science Institute produced twenty-three published books and scores of articles for professional journals. However, much of the research and many of the monographs produced from it were buried in the Institute's files. Interest in studying Negro history and culture was limited to a small coterie of scholars, located almost entirely in the South, most of whom were Negroes. Interest among the reading public was negligible. Fortunately, the Institute's files were preserved and are now deposited in the Amistad Research Center, along with other manuscript pieces relating to Negro life and history. The United Church Press is to be commended for rediscovering this material, recognizing its relevance to contemporary life, and making it available to socially aware readers.

The significance and originality of the Institute's research is well exemplified by the material in this volume. Permanently captured here is a segment of life that is uniquely American and, in spite of similarities to primitive religious experiences among whites, distinctively Negro. The narratives could not be recreated today by the most diligent research. The ex-slaves are gone, and the social and religious milieu out of which the conversions grew has drastically changed or—more accurately—disappeared entirely. Yet this environment was an important part of the folk history of the

Negro, and an awareness of it is necessary for understanding what is today commonly referred to by blacks as "soul." The authenticity with which the narratives and anecdotes portray both the ex-slaves and their environment is evident and results from the painstaking efforts of the researcher, Andrew Polk Watson. Mr. Watson made frequent visits to the homes of each person interviewed over a three-year period, questioning him for long periods of time. The autobiographical narratives were then culled from long and rambling accounts, but in most cases the conversion experiences were repeated several times as here recorded, with little or no variation from one telling to the next.

The value of these narratives, however, does not lie in their factual content or the accuracy of detail of the reminiscences, but in the tone or general mood they convey. In their introductory statements, Dr. Johnson and Dr. Radin have indicated the implications of the documents for sociologists, social psychologists, and students of religion and anthropology. For the historian the narratives have a twofold value. First, American history has been written largely from the point of view of the elite, the educated and articulate, who had the foresight to preserve historical records. The autobiographies printed here, in spite of the internal inconsistencies, ambiguities, and contradictions, vividly and quite comprehensively describe slavery as viewed by the unlettered and inarticulate slave. And if one is to understand how slavery and white racism have contributed to present-day American problems, one must begin with understanding what these facts of American life have meant to the Negro. Second, the narratives become primary sources for studying Southern Negro life in the 1920's. There is sufficient variety and repetition to provide the social historian with a broad basis for interpretation.

The narratives will have a particular value for the general reader interested in race relations. As folk history and folk literature they make enjoyable reading, but, more seriously, they demonstrate some of the elusive cultural differences between white and black America, caused by the proscriptions placed on the Negro, which complicate and often frustrate efforts at interracial cooperation.

Since there is no one Negro dialect, it was a wise choice to abandon efforts at dialect-writing in order to present the narratives in a more readable form. While preserving the idioms and expressive descriptive passages of the speakers, each narrative has a flow, unhindered by peculiar and unfamiliar phonetic spellings, and the entire collection has a unity of tone that could not have been achieved through strict adherence to the fine distinctions of the various dialects.

For this publication one significant addition has been made to the original manuscript of *God Struck Me Dead*. The essay by Mr. Watson, with its clear and unadorned description of religious services, serves to put the conversion experiences in the religious setting out of which they grew and helps to explain the vividness with which the experiences were recalled. Before an individual could participate at all in the religious services, which were so important in releasing the pent-up emotions of a dejected and rejected people, he must "come bringing the news of his resurrection from death and hell, and he had to bring it straight." There could be no doubt in the preacher's mind or among the congregation that he had been "borned again." The essay, written in 1932, is taken from Mr. Watson's unpublished Master of Arts thesis for the Fisk University department of anthropology. Mr. Watson is emeritus professor of social science at Wiley College in Marshall, Texas.

Clifton H. Johnson
Director
Amistad Research Center
Fisk University

Foreword

Status, Fantasy, and the Christian Dogma

A note about the conversion experiences of
Negro ex-slaves

To those interested in the history of the American Negro,
no period is of more vital importance than the development
following the Civil War. But to understand what then took
place, two questions must be answered: first, what was the
nature of the religious experience of the members of the older
generation; and second, what was the nature of the adaptation of the older Negroes, more specifically those who had
once been slaves, to the new order of things with which they
were faced. In order to make some contribution toward the
solution of these problems we collected two types of infor-
mation: a long series of conversion experiences, and a shorter
but fully representative series of autobiographies.

More than forty conversion experiences were obtained from
both men and women, varying considerably in length and
detail, and from their study it seems perfectly clear that
whether they represent a readaptation of a preexisting Christian pattern or not, to the older Negroes they could have
meant only one thing—a new individuation, an inward reintegration. It has always been an extremely strange fact that,
both during the days of slavery and during the first decade
after the war, so few individuals escaped complete demoralization and so few developed neuroses. It seems to me that we
shall find an explanation in the narratives that follow.

In the days of slavery, an adaptation to the external world
in which slaves lived was blocked completely except on a
very superficial level. Only in an inner world could the Negroes develop a scale of values and fixed points of vantage
from which to judge the world around them and themselves.

For those who had any marked spiritual cravings—and their number is assuredly as large in one race as another—even the best of masters could have little understanding. No respect was ever paid to the right of their emotions for an adequate outlet, for any outlet at all in fact. The vast majority of white people denied that they had any but the crudest kind of emotions to begin with. The inconsistent attempt to bring them into contact with the somewhat barren Christianity that prevailed in the antebellum South was, after all, only a cowardly surrogate for what they needed. What possible value could Christianity have for a people whose holiest human feelings were being daily and callously outraged? And this besmirchment—for besmirchment it was in every sense of the term—was bound to leave the victims with a sense of degradation and sin; to be sinned against is also to sin. And the sins from which the bewildered slave sought to be delivered when he made his prayer to the Christian God were only secondarily those of cardplaying, dancing, and fiddling. What he wanted was cleansing and its concomitant rebirth. To a man seeking a union with God it is immaterial how his soul has become befouled, and one can always rely upon an unanchored humility and a feeling of inferiority to discover that the suppliant has himself been responsible for the befoulment.

The Negro conversion experiences that follow conform to the normal pattern for all such experiences. They begin with a sense of sin and nonrealization and terminate with one of cleanliness, certainty, and reintegration, the three things every Negro was denied in life. What the slave desired was a status that he himself had ordained, not a fictitious one imposed from without. Such a status he could only secure in the realm of dreams, fantasies, and visions. We are not here dealing with the free fantasies of an artist or poet. Two forces definitely controlled and gave direction to this life of the imagination: the unconscious striving of all mature men and women for some form of harmony, and the organized and firm framework of Christian dogma. Any ordered framework would have done. That of Christianity happened to be at hand. So they used it, and the Christian God and Christian symbolism became their handmaids.

I do not feel that Christianity itself, the specific system of Christian dogma, made any appeal to them. There is very little mention of most of the cardinal dogmas of the Christian church. Even the dogma of the trinity is only vaguely reflected in the experiences and quite inadequately understood. The antebellum Negro was not converted to God. He converted God to himself. In the Christian God he found a fixed point, and he needed a fixed point, for both within and outside of himself he could see only vacillation and endless shifting. All that this God demanded was an unqualified faith and a throwing away of doubt. Amidst the uncertainties, the contradictions, and crises that surrounded the Negro, this is precisely what he wanted, and he gave his assent with joy and enthusiasm. Indeed, often he gave it with a jubilant hysteria. Doubt became the sin of sins. I remember only too well talking to an old Negro who had suffered unusual hardships as a slave, who thundered at me when I asked him how he could reconcile the treatment he had received from people professing to be Christians with a belief in the goodness of the Christian God. "Son," he roared, "I put that doubt behind me long ago!" It was well that he had, well that they all had. There was no other safety for people faced on all sides by doubt and the threat of personal disintegration, by the thwarting of instincts and the annihilation of values.

So here at last, in this combination of the natural striving for a unified personality and for a fixed God as the center of the world who would demand a nonrecalcitrant obedience and faith, a new world was forged. Small wonder then that he who achieved it could only visualize it as a rebirth, or that he could picture it as attainable only after many dangers had been successfully overcome, after one had literally been suspended over the very brink of hell. It must have been particularly difficult for such a race of realists as were the Negroes, for people so inextricably enmeshed in life as they were. Such individuals are never romanticists, nor do they often delude themselves by having recourse to simple and puerile wish fulfillments. Then, too, it must be remembered that they came from an unusually healthy and virile African strain. It would not have been enough to fool themselves. They had to convince themselves under conditions that were always more than likely to give the lie. So they had definitely to be struck down; conversion had to be in the nature of a stroke of lightning which would enter at the top of their head and emerge from their toes. They had to meet God, be baptized by him in the river of Jordan personally, become identified with him. Yet even after they had seen heaven and hell, even after they had heard the loveliest singing in the world, drunk from the same cup as the cherubim who surrounded the deity, they never became mystics. They kept on enjoying life and refused to retire from it. For this their sense of the realities was too great. After all, what they desired was status; when they had attained it, even if it was only an inward one, they could safely indulge in backsliding and sin, and yet not run too great a danger of personal disintegration.

In reading the conversions that follow it would be well to bear in mind, as I have already pointed out, that no matter how similar they are in general pattern and even in phraseology to white models, they are not mere imitations or an inert continuation of a white tradition. First of all I somewhat doubt whether the similarity is really as great as it is generally assumed to be, and second, even if it were, it must be remembered that the white Methodists or Baptists were good Christians with a fixed creed in which they were well-versed. What they were seeking to obtain was a specific kind of new Christian experience. It was a conversion to a new fellowship with Christ that they wished, not a rebirth. Failure meant no great hardship, and it most emphatically did not mean demoralization or disintegration. In fact, nothing fundamental was really at stake. As we have pointed out above, the case was quite different with the Negro slave, and this difference comes out very clearly when we see the marked degree to which the conversions among the white people early became stereotyped. There were, of course, numerous stereotyped formulas in the Negro conversions likewise, but the personality of the suppliant often played havoc with the pattern—not because his was a stronger personality, but because the purpose for which he sought God was so utterly different. The white Methodist or Baptist was asked to prove that Christ had forgiven his sins; the Negro Methodist or Baptist was asked to prove that Christ had recognized him and that he had recognized Christ. In fact, it was not so much the Negro who sought God as God who sought the Negro. The difficulty the latter experienced was how to recognize who was talking to him. In many instances the conversion experiences indicate quite clearly that God had literally to struggle with him, not to persuade him to give up his sins but to force him to be willing to express himself, to fulfill his mission—in other words, to attain individuation. The sins would take care of themselves.

When we turn to the autobiographies, we meet the same phenomenon in an entirely different setting. The war was over and the Negroes had been freed. The expression of the most fundamental human emotions could no longer be interfered with. Parents would no longer be torn from their children or children from their parents; women would no longer be outraged almost before the very eyes of their husbands and fathers. To this there was no difficulty for people to adjust themselves. No new problem was involved here. But new situations arose to which adjustment was absolutely imperative. How were they to support themselves in an inimical environment? Would the realization that they could now give free vent to all their feelings, good and bad, lead to spiritual and moral demoralization? It would have required a race of supermen not to go under, and many did go under. But a certain percentage did not: the same percentage, it may be surmised, who refused to succumb under the old order of things. It is from these individuals that the autobiographies were obtained. They were the only ones, naturally, who saw any unity and purpose in their lives. Doubtless their lives were not as interesting as the lives of those who became unanchored and who lost all values. But their story is far more important psychologically and humanly speaking. It gives the lie to the ill-natured prophecies that once delivered from the protection of his white masters the Negro would revert to the hypothetical barbarism from which he was supposed to have but recently emerged in Africa, and license would reign supreme. But what actually did happen? Those became demoralized who would generally become demoralized during transitional periods, while the vast majority sought to imitate the bourgeois civilization of their former white masters so far as their poverty permitted. A few achieved a new integration. It is with those few who succeeded in making a constructive adaptation to the new order of things and who were able to forge a new set of values that the autobiographies deal.

We cannot here enter into all the psychological implications with which the autobiographical narratives fairly bristle. That we must reserve for another place. They are all characteristically different. In the first we have the life history of a man of apparently great physical strength, an uncontrollable temper of which he was very proud, and a keen sense of humor. After a considerable period of dissipation that brought him almost to the state of complete demoralization he is converted and becomes the dullest of bourgeois. As a slave he had made a good adaptation to his environment, and this ability did not desert him when, under infinitely more difficult conditions, he was called upon to make another and more complete one.

In the second narrative we are dealing with a man of an entirely different temperament. The hero of our first autobiography was in no sense unusual. He was a typical, hard-headed, unemotional extrovert. His feelings were always respectable and never particularly profound. The hero of our second autobiography was the direct antithesis. To begin with, he was a thinking introvert with a very strong development of his feeling side. His whole life was colored by his strong attachment to his mother, and when he was sold south and separated from her, his only further interest in life was focused upon the possibility of seeing her again—if not in this world, at least in the next. He was deeply imbued with religion before he ever left home, and his subsequent conversion was, in large measure, not a new religious experience but a surrogate for the loss of his mother. He was a man of unusual intelligence, and by his temperament compelled to systematize and justify all his thoughts and feelings. He developed a full and rigid, if somewhat heterodox, theology and displayed unusual dialectical powers in defending it. A propagandist by nature, he was not happy unless he was converting other people to the faith. The one cardinal sin was doubt—doubt that there was a God and that he was good. Nothing that happened in the actual world really mattered. He gives a most harrowing picture of his sufferings under his second master, but he never for a moment felt that the goodness of God was to be questioned. As long as a person kept himself from disintegration in this world, he would be rewarded by the fullest kind of reintegration in the next. The key to his life was his love for his mother. Here there was no doubt: and God and his mother were one.

The autobiographies of the other six people are far less comprehensive than the first two. In fact, they are the merest of sketches. The individuals from whom they were obtained were quite definitely minor characters. Their ambitions had been moderate and had been adequately achieved. All of them had made excellent adaptations to the new life and looked back upon the past with surprisingly little bitterness. One of the outstanding facts that emerges is the extreme realism of the women. They had all had their conversion experience, and yet some remained doubters for a long time, while one was frankly indifferent. Apparently they were far more interested in finding an adequate and full expression for their emotional life in this world than in preparing for glory in the next.

Toward the end a number of dreams and visions have been included to show how they contrast with the more or less set patterns of the conversions proper.

Paul Radin

Contents

Introduction

The religious experiences illustrated in these documents are instances of the phenomenon commonly known as "conversion." A conversion experience—whether it be in religious or other form—is marked by a sudden and a striking "change of heart," with an abrupt change in the orientation of attitudes and beliefs. It is accompanied by what can be described as an "emotional regeneration, typically sudden in its advent and consummation." Conversion thus affects radically one's outlook toward life and one's conception of oneself.

It should be noted that the conversion experience is not limited to the world of the supernatural. Similar occurrences are observable in the lives of leaders of certain types of social reform movements. A sudden right-about-face is a common experience of radicals, reformers, and great prophets. Leaders and members of new sects, humanitarian cults, idealistic communities, and an array of esoteric movements of the more recent decades seem to undergo conversion experiences. Nonetheless, religious conversion is the commonest type: the Protestant Christian faith expects it, provides a means for the expression of one's inner struggle and conflict of values, and rewards one with dramatic expression by giving him certain status within the religious organization. Moreover, the conversion experience is not confined to a particular segment of the population, though it is more generally associated with adolescence. Indeed, conversion is not an experience unique to a single people or race, albeit it is more frequently associated with Negroes, mountain folk, and the "downtrodden poor." In other words, the conversion experience is a fairly general phenomenon, and it is because of this fact that the attention of students of the social sciences is focused upon it.

Because the conversion experience is an integral phase of the growth of individual personality, it can be said to fall within the orbit of social psychology. It is an event in the growth process of a person. That quality which by its very nature is intrinsically individual becomes meaningful when it is seen in the context of the development of the personality.

It is largely because conversion is an individual experience that it is generally incomprehensible to others who have not had a similar experience. There is, however, a considerable degree of uniformity in the cultural mode of expression of this type of individual inner struggle and conflict. The cultural and institutional context provides an individual with the pattern, norm, and form through which an inner emotional struggle may have personal expression. At the roots of most human emotional problems lie the conflicting demands and expectations germinating from a system of conflicting human relationships. All sociologically significant fears germinate from a precarious existence which is a result of these inharmonious relationships of persons and groups. The fear of losing one's affection-object, anxiety arising from fear of loss of status, and a whole array of emotional problems appear to be subjective manifestations of an objective world of conflicting values. Moreover, the very concepts and objects are culturally defined. Man fears because he is taught to be afraid of certain objects and certain conduct; he suffers a sense of guilt because he lives in a social world that teaches him to be sinless. Man is doubtless the only animal that experiences conversion, and when he does, he is within the definition and framework of a culture. Herein lies the uniformity of all conversion experiences.

Individuals whose conversion experiences are reproduced in these documents have gone through a dramatic experience —sudden sickness, blurring of vision, painful pressure of heart followed by "death" experiences (during which they see hell but are saved by the grace of God, or are shown a "big, glorious city" wherein resides a man who commands them to "go tell others of your experience.") Finally they are brought to life—or feel themselves to be reborn. Although each individual tells his death and rebirth in his own way and with his own artistic embellishment, there is a common thread that runs through all the documents. Visions, symbols, and rituals are permeated with the culture of our society, particularly with Christian dogmas and doctrines. This group of conversion experiences and autobiographies may well be regarded as "living documents" revealing the way an individual, having lived in the social world, makes that world a part of his own life organization.

The conversion experiences recorded in these documents and the autobiographical accounts of ex-slaves were gathered by A. P. Watson, a graduate student in anthropology in the years 1927–1929, under the guidance of Dr. Paul Radin, who was then serving as research professor of anthropology at Fisk University. A hundred individuals were interviewed, all of them older people, and their experiences, elicited only through extreme tact and sympathetic understanding, were written down exactly as they were obtained (except for very minor editing plus some modification of dialectic peculiarities to facilitate readability). In no instance was any attempt made to make these accounts any more literary than they actually were. The titles were selected by Dr. Radin and Mr. Watson, but they always refer to a striking phrase in the text itself.

Charles S. Johnson

Essay by Andrew P. Watson

negro primitive religious services

Religious ceremonies among the Negro primitive Baptists in central Tennessee are very exclusive, certainly in regard to "sinners." Their services are for the "formed of God," and not for the sinner. He can have no part in such worship—no, not even to pray. Nor is there any debate over one's status and rights to join in the ceremonies, for one either has or has not been "borned again." Even though one may feel that he is a sheep "from the foundation of the world," he stands condemned until this "time-God" wills to free his soul. "What God condemns I condemn and pity not," says Mrs. A. The best a sinner can do, therefore, is come into these gatherings and see the saints shout and rejoice and wait until his change comes. This change may come just in time for one to make a deathbed confession. But even at this the individual is reckoned as having died a sheep; and hence has gone to ."shout around the throne of God." It was decreed before the foundation of the world that he should be dealt with in this way. He was born into the world to be a sheep, but God did not will to reveal himself to him until the last minute.

The case of the sinner has been aptly stated in numerous sermons. A few thoughts from one of such sermons delivered by Reverend H. follow:

A sinner is dead, but we borned of God are live children. No dead child can understand the works of a live one, because he ain't had his eyes opened. This nobody can do but God. If God don't open your blinded eyes, cut loose your stammering tongue, unstop your deaf ears, and deliver your soul from death and hell, you are dead and can't understand the things we do. You got to be dug up, rooted and grounded, and buried in him. When this has been done, you are an "elect" and you will come bringing the news. There's no maybes about it, for if he has ever freed your soul you will know it. For he never leaves none of his children in ignorance.

This indifferent, if not hostile, attitude is not manifested toward sinners only, but communicants of other denominations as well. That is, unless such persons can tell about "that morning when my dungeons shook and my chains fell off." At times the reference to others is pointed and plain, while at other times the attitude can be gleaned from some such expressions as the following: "You talk about your Bible religion; I know nothing about it. But I got a home over yonder from everlasting to everlasting and know it." And again, "You can fool folks here in this world, but none goin' to enter into that city over yonder but them that's truly borned of God. This handshaking, Bible religion is nothing. You got to have it in the heart, and if God don't put the grace there it won't get there."[1]

A Typical Sunday Meeting

A visit to one of the churches, especially in the rural section, reveals that gatherings here have great social as well as religious significance. On Sundays when services are to be held, the congregation gathers long before it is time to begin. As they drop in one or two at a time, there is much merriment. Each new arrival means a round of handshaking and earnest

[1] Lest there should be some misunderstanding: It is not my intention to convey the impression that Negro primitive Baptists carry hatred in their hearts against other people and denominations. This behavior described above might more aptly be styled a "defense or compensatory mechanism." To see the reasonableness of this explanation it need only be remembered that many if not most of these people are illiterate. In order to make up for this shortcoming they make claim of an overdose of "heartfelt religion." "Book learning, while good, is worldly and got nothing to do with being borned of God," said Mrs. A one day.

inquiry as to health. The greatest sympathy is expressed for the slightest misfortune. The news of the continued illness of some brother, sister, or friend may well call forth such words as the following: "The Master is keeping him here for some purpose," or, "His time just hasn't come." As the time nears for the services to begin the men take seats on their side of the pulpit.

After all have apparently gathered, but while the talking may yet be in full sway, one of the brethren may "raise a hymn." Soft and low at first, it becomes louder and louder as one after another joins in. Finally no talking can be heard. The whole congregation may join in the singing. Whereas a few minutes ago there was laughter and merriment, the whole situation is now changed; not a smile can be seen. The same hymn may last for ten or fifteen minutes. Along toward the end the preacher may rise and signal the congregation to follow his example. Then follows a round of handshaking and possibly shouting. The members file by the pulpit, shake the preacher's hand, and then return to their seats so as to pass each other, that all may shake hands. When shaking hands they look each other squarely in the eye. There is never a smile or movement that might detract from the seriousness with which the atmosphere by this time is supercharged.

Immediately following the song one of the members, usually male, is called upon to lead in prayer. Such a one takes a kneeling position before his seat. Sometimes all may do this, but for the most part the others bow their heads and cover their faces with their hands.

The prayer which follows may be taken as typical, though it was delivered on the occasion of a special meeting and by a deacon who has a wide reputation for being a man who "knows how to ring up heaven."[2]

Almighty and all-wise God, our heavenly Father! 'tis once more and again that a few of your beloved children are gathered together to call upon your holy name.

[2] This prayer was offered by a deacon during a camp-meeting held in South Nashville, Tennessee, in the summer of 1928. It is reproduced here as accurately as possible from the notes taken during the occasion.

We bow at your footstool, Master, to thank you for our spared lives. We thank you that we were able to get up this morning clothed in our right mind. For, Master, since we met here, many have been snatched out of the land of living and hurled into eternity. But through your goodness and mercy we have been spared to assemble ourselves here once more to call upon a Captain who has never lost a battle. Oh, throw round us your strong arms of protection. Bind us together in love and union. Build us up where we are torn down, and strengthen us where we are weak. O Lord! O Lord! take the lead of our minds, place them on heaven and heavenly divine things. O God, our Captain and King, search our hearts, and if you find anything there contrary to your divine will just move it from us, Master, as far as the east is from the west. Now Lord, you know our hearts, you know our hearts' desire. You know our downsitting and you know our uprising. Lord, you know all about us because you made us. Lord! Lord! One more kind favor I ask of you. Remember the man that is to stand in the gateway and proclaim your Holy Word. Oh, stand by him. Strengthen him where he is weak and build him up where he is torn down. Oh, let him down into the deep treasures of your word.

And now, O Lord, when this your humble servant is done down here in this lowland of sorrow; done sitting down and getting up; done being called everything but a child of God; oh, when I am done, done, done, and this old world can afford me a home no longer, right soon in the morning, Lord, right soon in the morning, meet me down at the river of Jordan, bid the waters to be still, tuck my little soul away in that snow-white chariot, and bear it away over yonder in the third heaven where every day will be a Sunday and my sorrows of this old world will have an end, is my prayer for Christ my Redeemer's sake and amen and thank God.

During the prayer the preacher and congregation mingled their voices with that of the petitioner in perfect cadence. "Oh, help him, Jesus." "Amen, amen." "Pray with him, children." "Oh, call upon his holy name." "Grant it, almighty God."

Immediately following the prayer another hymn is sung. Usually by this time—depending largely on the "rousement" of the prayer—there is much excitement and "shouting." The spirit is moving. As it "moves upon the main altar of the heart," the individual affected behaves according to temperament. This behavior may consist of leaping from bench to bench, jumping up and down in one's tracks, screaming, clapping the hands, crying, or any number of other movements with various contortions of the body. Often fellow members are victims of none too friendly blows from the hand of the "shouter." No one is supposed to take offense, however, for it is not the individual but "the spirit which worketh all things."

At the close of this hymn and while it may yet be almost impossible to hear what is being said for the "shouting," the preacher takes his place. After reading from the scriptures he leads another hymn, and then he begins his sermon. Often the "shouting" continues unceasingly throughout the services.

The Sermon

The average sermon can be divided into three parts. The first part usually consists of an apology on the part of the speaker for a cold, hoarseness, or some other infirmity. The second part may be styled the "warming-up" period. During this phase the preacher speaks from the scriptures and on the whole presents a sound argument, making practical applications to everyday life. All this time he is calling upon the members, saying, "Pray with me a little while, children," etc. He is feeling his way until the spirit strikes him. With the coming of the spirit, which is the third part of the sermon, the speaker's entire demeanor changes. He now launches into a type of discourse that borders on hysteria. His voice, changed in pitch, takes on a mournful, singing quality, and words flow from his lips in such a manner as to make an understanding of them almost impossible. Several visits were made to a certain church in Nashville where this division between the second

and third stages of the sermon was marked to an almost un-
believable degree. The transition is so strikingly dramatic
that one almost imagines that he sees the spirit as it envelops
the preacher. He suddenly breaks off in his discourse and lifts
his eyes toward the ceiling. Then, with one hand raised above
his head and the other trembling by his side, he stands for a
few seconds as if in great awe. Then, as though oblivious to
what he may have been saying a few seconds before, he
launches into the mysterious. A sermon which may be considered typical and which embodies all the above elements
follows:

Brothers and sisters, being a duty-bound servant of
God, I stand before you tonight. I am a little hoarse from
a cold. But if you will bear with me a little while we
will try to bring you a message of "thus sayeth the
Lord." If God is willing, we will preach. The hellhounds
are so swift on our trail that we have to go sometime
whether we feel like it or not. So we are here tonight to
hear what the spirit has to say.

My text is found in the X chapter and the Y verse.[3]
These words the Master spoke because he foresaw that a
time would come when men would not hear the true
word. It always makes my heart glad when I run back
in my mind and see what a powerful God this is we
serve. And every child—pray with me a little while,
children—that has been borned of the spirit, I mean
born until he can feel it, ought to feel proud that he is
serving a captain who has never lost a battle, a God that
can speak and man live, but utter his voice and man lay
down and die. A God that controls the muttering
thunders and makes the zigzag lightning play across the
heaven. Oh, ain't he a powerful God?

---

[3] Observations reveal that there is no truth in the popular
belief that these preachers always take their text from the Old
Testament. It is true, however, that they do not "stick to the
text." But this is due to the "spirit."

He stepped out on the slope of time one morning and declared, "I am God, and there's none like me. I'm God and there is none before me. In my own appointed time I will visit the iniquities of the earth. I will cut down on the right and on the left. But a remnant I will save." Ain't you glad then, children, that he always spares a remnant?

Brothers (pray with me a little while), we must gird up our loins. We who are born of the spirit should cling close to the Master, for he has promised to be a shelter in the time of storm, a rock in a weary land. Listen at him when he says, "Behold I lay in Zion, a stone, a tried stone." What need have we to worry about earthly things? They are temporal and will fade away. But we, the born of God, have laid hold on everlasting life. Every child that has had his soul delivered from death and hell (pray with me, brothers) and stayed at hell's dark door until he got his orders is a traveler. His home is not in this world. He is but a sojourner in a weary land.

Brothers! this being true we ought to love one another; we ought to be careful how we entertain strangers. If your neighbor mistreats you, do good for evil. For away by and by our God that sees all we do and hears all we say will come, and woe be unto him that has offended one of these his little ones. I know the way gets awful dark sometimes and it looks like everything is against us, but listen what Job said, "All the days of my appointed time I will wait on the Lord till my change comes!"

Sometimes we wake up in the dark hours of midnight, briny tears flowing down our cheeks (ah, pray with me a little longer, brothers). We cry and don't know what we are crying about. Brother, if you have been truly snatched from the greedy jaws of hell, your feet taken out of the miry clay and placed on the rock, the sure foundation, you will shed tears sometime. You just feel like you want to run away somewhere. But listen at the Master when he says, "Be still and know that I am God.

I have heard your groans, but I will not put on you a burden you cannot bear." We ought to rejoice and be glad, for while they think, we know we have been born of God because we have felt his power, tasted his love, waited at hell's dark door for orders, and got a through ticket straight through from hell to heaven. We have seen the travel of our soul. He dressed us up, told us we were his children, sent us back into this lowland of sorrows to tarry until one sweet day when he shall send the angel of death to bear our soul from this old earthly tabernacle back home to glory—I say back home, because we been there once and ever since that day we have been making our way back.

During this time shouts have been coming from all sections of the "Amen Corners": "Preach, boy! Yes, my God! Goin' rise with healing in my wings that morning." It is at this point that the spirit strikes the preacher. He now launches into the mysterious.

Brothers! Aha! Glory to God! The Captain is on board now, brothers. Sit still and hear the word of God, aha; away back, away back brothers, aha! Before the wind ever blowed, aha! Before the flying clouds, aha! Or before ever the earth was made, aha! our God had us in mind. Ha! Oh, brothers; oh, brothers! Ha! Ain't you glad then, aha! that our God, ha! looked down through time that morning, aha! saw me and you, aha! ordained from the very beginning that we should be his children, aha! the work of his almighty hand, aha!

Old John the Revelator, aha! a-looking over yonder, aha! in bright glory, aha! "Oh, what do you see, John?" Ha! "I see a number, aha! A great number, aha! A host that no man can number, aha!" "Who are these, aha!" I heard the angel Gabriel when he answered, aha! "These are they that come up through hard trials and great tribulations, aha! who washed their robes, aha! and made them white in the blood of the lamb, aha! They are now shouting around the throne of God, aha!"

Well, oh, brothers! Oh, brothers! Ain't you glad that

you have already been in the dressingroom, had your everlasting garments fitted on, and sandals on your feet? We born of God, aha! are shod for traveling, aha! Oh, glory to God! It won't be long before some of us here, aha! will bid farewell, aha! take the wings of the morning, aha! where there'll be no more sin and sorrow, aha! no more weeping and mourning, aha! We can just walk around, brother, aha! go over and shake hands with old Moses, aha! see Father Abraham, aha! talk with Peter, Matthew, Luke, and John, aha! And, oh yes, glory to God! we will want to see our Savior, the Lamb that was slain, ha! They tell me that his face outshines the sun, aha! but we can look on him, aha! because we will be like him. And then, oh, brother, oh, brother, we will just fly from cherubim to cherubim. There with the angels we will eat off the welcome table, aha! Soon! Soon, we will all be gathered together over yonder. Brothers, ain't you glad you done died the sinner-death and don't have to die no more? When we rise to fly that morning, we can fly with healing in our wings.

Now, if you don't hear my voice no more, aha! remember, I am a Hebrew child, aha! Just meet me over yonder, aha! on the other side of the river of Jordan, away back in the third heaven.

By this time more than a dozen persons are "shouting"— some merely wringing their hands, others jumping, crying, or walking from member to member mourning and saying, "I am so glad; I am so glad."

At the close of the sermon two or three deacons gather around a table and, after prompting some of the sisters or brothers to lead a hymn, they proceed to "raise collection." This is done by calling upon everyone "what's got anything to give to come forward and lay it on the table," or announcing, "If you don't feel like moving, just raise your hand and we will wait on you." This period of the services is usually welcomed by many of the young visitors, for it gives the young women a chance to express themselves by walking to the table and showing off some recently acquired garment.

Usually a second hymn must be sung for the deacons to "even up" the money. This may call for a few pennies in order to make sixty cents a dollar, or a dollar or more to make an even five or ten. The demands at any time will depend upon the need for money, the size of the audience, and the nature of the sermon just delivered. Hardly ever will the deacons stop until they have raised the additional amount, whatever it be. After it has been secured and counted, one of the deacons faces the audience and says, "Thank the congregation for _____ dollars. The Lord loves a cheerful giver."

The preacher then rises and, after reminding the congregation of the sick members and urging the "well to visit the sick," or reminding them of prayer-meeting night, he says the benediction. Then follows much handshaking and many farewells. "If you don't see me no more in this world, just remember that I am a sheep. I got a home over yonder, and none goin' see me but the borned of God."[4]

Shouting

Much has been said above about "shouting." This is done by both men and women, and may happen at any time or place. It all depends upon the spirit. The "shouter" may go through one or all of the movements pointed out above, depending on his feeling at the time or his customary way of behaving. Indeed, there is a great deal of individuality displayed in "shouting." The members of any given church know the characteristic movements of each individual shouter of the group. For instance, in a certain church in Nashville, there is one man who shouts by leaping from one bench to another over the heads of his fellow worshipers. No one ever attempts to hold him, nor does he fail to get the right-of-way.

[4] In rural districts, where such gatherings are few and where many have come together on some special occasion, these farewells are said in such a way as to leave no doubt as to their sincerity. Indeed, it might seem that many say farewell half hoping, at least, that they will not meet again in this life. It is "in that land over yonder" that they want to meet.

Many of these worshipers have tried to explain the feelings which prompt them to shout. Two or three illustrations follow:

"I shout because there is a fire on the inside. When I witness the truth, the fire moves on the main altar of my heart, and I can't keep still." Another says, "We children of God shout because of that love that wells up in our bosom. It is that love which runs from heart to heart and from breast to breast. We have to cry out." Mr. G. explains it thus: "Shouting is but the outward manifestation of an inward joy."

But in spite of this joy, there is often an element of sorrow. For instance, many people have been observed to shout when told of some great calamity, as the sinking of a ship, or death and destruction caused by a flood, cyclone, or any natural phenomenon. Others have been observed to shout when telling of their past life and conversion. "I shout when I think of the hard road I have traveled," says Mrs. H.

Often there is shouting at funerals. This may happen even in cases where the deceased died a "sinner," and hence left considerable doubt as to "which way he went." The words uttered while the individual is shouting give the best index to feelings here. Such expressions as the following may often be heard: "My God is cutting on the right and on the left." "My God done fixed it so the rich must die as well as the poor." "None going in that building but the truly borned of God."[5]

---

[5] Funerals are always occasions for great gatherings. The usual singing followed by prayer takes place. After this the obituary is read, and then the preacher or preachers—usually there are several—rise and speak briefly on the life of the deceased. They usually begin with God away back in the council-room, looking down "through time before time." There he foresaw and decreed this very occasion. After this, not much else is said about the deceased, for "if he was a sheep, he's gone on in the building; but if he was a goat, hell is his home, and he is now lifting up his eyes in torment." There are no "ifs" and "ands" about it. Hence they do not dwell on this at length. This is God's work and he says, "Judge not." For these and other reasons sermons here often do not differ but little from those delivered on other occasions.

On the other hand, should the deceased be one of the saints, the shout takes on more of the color of joy. "It is heaven's gain," the shouter may say, or, "Thank God, another elect has been taken out of this lowland of sorrows. He's gone and is now shut up in the building and shouting around the throne of God."

A few lines from one or two spirituals furnished during an interview will show the attitude on an occasion of this kind:

> Just as soon as I am done with my trials here,
> With my trials, with my trials here;
> Just as soon as I am done,
> I'm going home to live with the angels.

Or this one:

> Oh, brother (sister), ain't you glad
> That we 'most done traveling?
> Going to carry my soul to the Lord.
>
> It's a mighty rocky road
> But I'm 'most done traveling.
> Going to carry my soul to the Lord.

Shouting as described here is not to be confused with the "holy dance." Such of these dances as have been observed are group affairs and have specified places in the ceremony. In most cases there are instruments, and the dancers move and sway to the music and singing. Shouting, on the other hand, is a spontaneous act, and may happen any time the individual feels the spirit. "It's the fire on the inside, and we can't keep still," is one of the explanations offered above. To make the distinction clear: in the "holy dance" the aim, it would seem, is to work it down.

But in order to better understand this expression of religion set forth in the above description, let us turn to the concepts of God and the individual accounts of conversion.

Prologue

a man in a man

I am too old to preach now, and I spend my time in sweet contemplation and peaceful meditation on the wondrous works of God.

I was a slave when converted. Before that I used to swear a great deal and do many things which caused my master to whip me a lot. At times I would go to hear preaching among the slaves, not to be converted however, but mainly to hear the moaning and hear the preacher quote the scriptures. Often, while at work, I tried to go through the motions and intonations of the preacher. I was pretty good at heart but considered a devil by those around me.

Son, you have asked me to speak of God. Who is God? God is a spirit and seeks only those to worship him who will worship in spirit and truth.

What do I mean? I mean, son, that all the reading in the world will not help you. Unless God opens up your understanding and reveals his mighty works to you, you are dead. God has promised to those who serve him eternal life. Thus if you are dead you have no part with him. We judge a tree by the fruit it bears. A good tree cannot bring forth corrupt fruit. We must get right on the inside before we can get right on the outside, and we only reach this stage when God, through his mercy, has compassion on us and frees our souls from hell—for we are conceived in iniquity and born in sin.

How can we find God? God has a chosen people. He has always had a chosen people, and he calls whomsoever he wills. Any child who has been born of the spirit knows it, for he has felt God's power, tasted his love, and seen the travel of his own soul. God chastises his children for their disobedience. This body of ours is but a temple, and like any other house it is nothing without occupants.

There is a man in a man. The soul is the medium between God and man. God speaks to us through our conscience, and the reasoning is so loud that we seem to hear a voice. But if God gave us the power of speech, can he not talk? If a soul calls on God, having no other earthly hope, will God not reveal himself to such a one? Is he asleep? Is he not merciful, and is he not long-suffering? He is a true God, working all things after the counsel of his own will. We must trust him for our journey and thank him for our daily bread and for our spared lives.

God looked down through the scope of time and saw every generation, even down to this day. Then God conceived the idea of making man. He stooped down and took a handful of clay. But the earth mourned, and God made a contract with the earth saying, "Weep not, for lo! I will repay every atom." Thus, when we die, our bodies go back to Mother Earth and the soul to the God that giveth. Those who have been born of the spirit will be welcomed back into the house of God, but those who have not been killed dead and made alive again in Christ Jesus, who have not been dug up and rooted and grounded and buried in the Lord, they will have their portion in outer darkness. This must be so, for not one iota of sin can enter that haven of rest.

There is a real heaven and hell. The hell is the devil and his angels. They are evil spirits and are ever present with us to tempt and try us. They are at war with the heavenly host and seek to dissuade those who would serve God.

i am
blessed
but you are
damned

One day while in the field plowing I heard a voice. I jumped because I thought it was my master coming to scold and whip me for plowing up some more corn. I looked but saw no one. Again the voice called, "Morte! Morte!" With this I stopped, dropped the plow, and started running, but the voice kept on speaking to me saying, "Fear not, my little one, for behold! I come to bring you a message of truth."

Everything got dark, and I was unable to stand any longer. I began to feel sick, and there was a great roaring. I tried to cry and move but was unable to do either. I looked up and saw that I was in a new world. There were plants and animals, and all, even the water where I stooped down to drink, began to cry out, "I am blessed but you are damned! I am blessed but you are damned!" With this I began to pray, and a voice on the inside began to cry, "Mercy! Mercy! Mercy!"

As I prayed an angel came and touched me, and I looked new. I looked at my hands and they were new; I looked at my feet and they were new. I looked and saw my old body suspended over a burning pit by a small web like a spider web. I again prayed, and there came a soft voice saying, "My little one, I have loved you with an everlasting love. You are this day made alive and freed from hell. You are a chosen vessel unto the Lord. Be upright before me, and I will guide you unto all truth. My grace is sufficient for you. Go, and I am with you. Preach the gospel, and I will preach with you. You are henceforth the salt of the earth."

I then began to shout and clap my hands. All the time, a voice on the inside was crying, "I am so glad! I am so glad!" About this time an angel appeared before me and said with a loud voice, "Praise God! Praise God!" I looked to the east, and there was a large throne lifted high up, and thereon sat one, even God. He looked neither to the right nor to the left. I was afraid and fell on my face. When I was still a long way off I heard a voice from God saying, "My little one, be not afraid, for lo! many wondrous works will I perform through thee. Go in peace, and lo! I am with you always." All this he said but opened not his mouth while speaking. Then all those about the throne shouted and said, "Amen."

I then came to myself again and shouted and rejoiced. After so long a time I recovered my real senses and realized that I had been plowing and that the horse had run off with the plow and dragged down much of the corn. I was afraid and began to pray, for I knew the master would whip me most unmercifully when he found that I had plowed up the corn.

About this time my master came down the field. I became very bold and answered him when he called me. He asked me very roughly how I came to plow up the corn, and where the horse and plow were, and why I had got along so slowly. I told him that I had been talking with God Almighty, and that it was God who had plowed up the corn. He looked at me very strangely, and suddenly I fell for shouting, and I shouted and began to preach. The words seemed to flow from my lips. When I had finished I had a deep feeling of satisfaction and no longer dreaded the whipping I knew I would get. My master looked at me and seemed to tremble. He told me to catch the horse and come on with him to the barn. I went to get the horse, stumbling down the corn rows. Here again I became weak and began to be afraid for the whipping. After I had gone some distance down the rows, I became dazed and again fell to the ground. In a vision I saw a great mound and, beside it or at the base of it, stood the angel Gabriel. And a voice said to me, "Behold your sins as a great mountain. But they shall be rolled away. Go in peace, fearing no man, for lo! I have cut loose your stammering tongue and unstopped your deaf ears. A witness shalt thou be, and thou shalt speak to multitudes, and they shall hear. My word has gone forth, and it is power. Be strong, and lo! I am with you even until the world shall end. Amen."

I looked, and the angel Gabriel lifted his hand, and my sins, that had stood as a mountain, began to roll away. I saw them as they rolled over into a great pit. They fell to the bottom, and there was a great noise. I saw old Satan with a host of his angels hop from the pit, and there they began to stick out their tongues at me and make motions as if to lay hands on me and drag me back into the pit. I cried out, "Save me! Save me, Lord!" And like a flash there gathered around me a host of angels, even a great number, with their backs to me and their faces to the outer world. Then stepped one in the direction of the pit. Old Satan and his angels, growling with anger and trembling with fear, hopped back into the pit. Finally again there came a voice unto me saying, "Go in peace and fear not, for lo! I will throw around you a strong arm of protection. Neither shall your oppressors be able to confound you. I will make your enemies feed you and those who despise you take you in. Rejoice and be exceedingly glad, for I have saved you through grace by faith, not of yourself but as a gift of God. Be strong and fear not. Amen."

I rose from the ground shouting and praising God. Within me there was a crying, "Holy! Holy! Holy is the Lord!"

I must have been in this trance for more than an hour. I went on to the barn and found my master there waiting for me. Again I began to tell him of my experience. I do not recall what he did to me afterwards. I felt burdened down and that preaching was my only relief. When I had finished I felt a great love in my heart that made me feel like stooping and kissing the very ground. My master sat watching and listening to me, and then he began to cry. He turned from me and said in a broken voice, "Morte, I believe you are a preacher. From now on you can preach to the people here on my place in the old shed by the creek. But tomorrow morning, Sunday, I want you to preach to my family and neighbors. So put on your best clothes and be in front of the big house early in the morning, about nine o'clock."

I was so happy that I did not know what to do. I thanked my master and then God, for I felt that he was with me. Throughout the night I went from cabin to cabin, rejoicing and spreading the news.

The next morning at the time appointed I stood up on two planks in front of the porch of the big house and, without a Bible or anything, I began to preach to my master and the people. My thoughts came so fast that I could hardly speak fast enough. My soul caught on fire, and soon I had them all in tears. I told them that God had a chosen people and that he had raised me up as an example of his matchless love. I told them that they must be born again and that their souls must be freed from the shackles of hell.

Ever since that day I have been preaching the gospel and am not a bit tired. I can tell anyone about God in the darkest hour of midnight, for it is written on my heart. Amen.

hooked
in the
heart

Before God can use a man, that man must be hooked in the heart. By this I mean that he has to feel converted. And once God stirs up a man's pure mind and makes him see the folly of his ways, he is wishing for God to take him and use him. From this time on it is up to God, and if he has ever started a work he will not stop until it is finished, and finished once and for all times. He spoke to me once after I had prayed trying to hurry him and get a religion. He said, "I am a time-God. Behold, I work after the counsel of my own will, and in due time I will visit whomsoever I will."

He showed me many things before he turned me around and then gave me my orders. I was a great musician, and at times, after I had spent seasons at fasting and praying, I would get tired of it and go back to the ways of the world. You see, the devil knows how to tempt a man. He always reminds him of the things he likes best, and in this way he can get his attention.

God started on me when I was a little boy. I used to grieve a lot over my mother. She had been sold away from me and taken a long way off. One evening I was going through the woods to get the cows. I was walking along thinking about Mama and crying. Then a voice spoke to me and said, "Blessed art thou. An obedient child shall live out the fullness of his days." I got scared because I did not know who it was that spoke nor what he meant. But from this time on I thought more about God and my soul and started to praying as best I knew how. It went on this way until I was about grown. I would pray awhile and then stop and forget God. Finally one day I was plowing in a field. There was a stump at one end, and as I came to the end and turned the team around I heard a mourning behind the stump. I turned around and sat on the plowhandle and looked, but didn't see anything. Yet the voice kept on mourning. I went on about my plowing, feeling sad and wondering what it all meant. The voice said nothing, but just mourned. Later God revealed to me that it was my soul crying out for deliverance. The voice was within me all the time, but it sounded like it was behind the stump. From this time on he began to show me things.

Once while I was sick I saw in a vision three people, and one was a woman. They looked at me and said, "He is sick." The woman said, "I can cure him." So speaking she took out a little silver vial, held it before me, and vanished.

At another time I saw myself traveling down a big, broad road. I came to three marks across my path, and it was revealed to me that those marks represented the number of times I had started to find God and turned back.

After this, one day, I was putting a top on our little log house that I was building. It was broad open day, and I was as wide awake as ever I was in this world. I had just got in position to fit on the first rafters when a voice called my name three distinct times. It called, "Oh, William! Oh, William! Oh, William!" I hollered and answered, "Hey!" But nobody answered. I looked all around and began to wonder about the voice. It sounded so strange. It seemed to come from afar off, and still it seemed to be right at me. I never have been able to find out what it meant.

I started to praying again. That night I went to my regular praying place. I usually prayed behind a big beech tree a little distance from the house, and often during the night, when I would feel to pray, I would get out of bed and go to this tree. That night I said, "Lord, if I am praying right, let me hear a dove mourn three times." While I was praying I went off in a trance, and I saw myself going up a broad, hilly road through the woods. When I was nearly to the top I saw a big dog. I got scared and started to run back, but something urged me on. The dog was chained to a big block, I found out when I got closer, and though she tried to get to me, I passed out of her reach. I came then to a tree like a willow, and there I heard a dove mourn three times.

But in spite of this it wasn't long before I was serving the devil again. I was serving him outwardly, but my soul was pleading with God. I turned back several times because the devil stayed so hot on my trail. Whenever a man tries to do right and seek God, then the devil gets busy. I used to go to my praying place, and it just looked like the devil would take me whether or no. I would see him with my spiritual eye as some great monster coming down out of the tree to tear me to pieces and devour me. Or else I would recall all the good times I had had. Such temptations are the first that a man goes through before he becomes purified and fit for God's kingdom.

You can't serve two masters. You either got to be on the one side or the other. Before any man hires another to work for him he tries to find out something about that man—what kind of a worker he is, how much interest he will take in his work, and how much time he can give. If that man finds out that you cannot give his job the proper time and interest, he can't use you no matter how good a worker you may be. The same is true with God. If we don't meet his requirements, he can't use us. He calls us and gives us our orders, and until a man gets orders from God he is not ready to serve him.

When God called me I had applied in hell, but my name wasn't on the roll. I saw a sharp-eyed looking man, and he seemed to be walking back and forth from one end of a workshop to the other and looking at a time book. I went to ask him if my name was in the book, and he snapped back, "No!" It was from here that God delivered my soul, turned me around, and gave me my orders. I saw myself on the same broad road I had seen so much of in the spirit. As I went along, a voice called out, "Oh, William! Oh, William! Oh, William!" When he said that he turned me around out of the big road into a little path, my face being toward the east. He spoke again and said, "Go preach my gospel to every creature and fear not, for I am with you, an everlasting prop. Amen."

my
jaws
became
unlocked

About twelve years before I got converted I was in a crap game out on the Harding Pike. I'll never forget it as long as I live. I and three or four others were gambling. I had the dice in my hands. A voice spoke to me, and it spoke three times. Every time it got nearer and nearer, until it seemed right over the top of my head. It said, "Have you ever thought where you will spend eternity?" I got sorrowful and sad and slipped out of the room and prayed. It was on the fifth day of October that I made a determination to follow the Lord. I saw him through the eye of faith and heard his voice through the spiritual ear until the heart understood.

Sometime after this—it was in June—my wife and mother-in-law were sitting in the room, and I was in the bed sick. A hand came and struck me across the face three times. Then I looked and saw the very gates of heaven open and an angel come out. It flew right to my bed and said, "I am a doctor that cures all diseases." That same day I got up and dressed myself and walked for the first time in three months.

I believe in the Baptist church, because before I was sure I joined the Missionary Baptist church. One day when I was standing between these walnut trees—this was three weeks before I joined church—I heard the Lord, and he spoke to me, and I saw him take a sun out of a sun, and he said to me, "Behold, my little one. I am God Almighty. I freed your soul from death and hell. I set you in Babylon until you knew that I ordained you to preach the gospel to every creature." I didn't know what this meant. For a long time I could not spiritually call on the name of the Lord. In 1906 I prayed for six months. God showed me what I was to do, and to my complaint that I was from a poor tribe and had no learning and had not had the advantages of other people he answered in a voice, "I am wisdom and possess all knowledge. I ordain you to preach."

Wisdom in the heart is unlike wisdom in the mind. There is but one way and that is the right way, and if I trust in God he never lets me fail.

I remember the first sermon I was to preach. I picked out two verses from the scripture and practiced on them as my text. But when I got up to preach, I started off all right but died dead right in the middle. I couldn't so much as call the name of the Lord. Then all at once I began to feel sorrowful, and my jaws became unlocked, and my tongue started to move so I could speak. I preached with no trouble, for I just said what the spirit directed me to say. This is why I don't prepare any sermons today. I just read the word and pray. God will do the rest.

Once I was called to preach when I had rheumatism in my leg. My wife hobbled all along the way to church with me, telling me all the time that I should have stayed home in bed, but I told her that I must fill my hand. The rest is the Lord's. I felt awful bad when I first got to church and took my place on the stand, waiting for the congregation to gather. And then the spirit lifted me up. I forgot all about the pain and just lost sight of the world and all the things of the world. When the spirit begins to work with one it don't have any cares for pain or anything of the world. My mind gets fixed on God and I feel a deep love, joy, and desire to be with God. We shout because we feel glad in the heart. At times I feel like I could just kiss the very feet of man, and I had rather hear the voice on the inside cry out "Amen" when I do something than to have all the money in the world. We rejoice because the spirit makes us feel so good and makes us forget all worldly cares.

the slave
who
joined
the yanks

I am about eighty-four years old and was born in Davidson County, a slave. The people that owned me came from Richmond, Virginia. There were three brothers of them, and they all had adjoining property.

I used to be awfully high-tempered even when I was a boy. My mistress and Mars' Bill kept my back sore from whipping because I fought so much. In them days all the children were called little mistress or little marster, and their parents used to tell me that I shouldn't hit or fight them. But every time they crossed me I jumped them. I just couldn't help it. I worked around the house all the time, and this made me be around them a lot. I had to get up in the morning, around four o'clock —I guessed the time by the stars—and blow the horn for the hands to get up and go feed. Then I would make fires, bring the water, milk the cows, get the horses ready for school, sweep, and help clean up the house. Along about six o'clock I would have to go in and waken Mars' Bill, Ole Missey, and Little Mistress.

One Saturday morning Little Missey was sleeping late. She did not have to go to school. Ole Missey told me to go and make up her bed. I went in, and she didn't want to get up so that I could make the bed. I told her then that it was late, and that Ole Missey said for her to get up. Then she got mad, jumped up in the bed, and said, "You black dog, get out of here. I'll get up when I get ready." With that she slapped me as hard as she could, right in my face. I saw stars. As soon as

I got back to myself I swung at her, and if she hadn't been so quick I would have almost killed her, for I hit at her with my fist and with all the force I had. I was just about ready to jump up on the bed and choke the life out of her when Ole Missey happened in. She told Ole Missey that I had snatched the cover off the bed and sassed her. Ole Missey turned on me and said, "What do you mean, you black devil? I'll strap your back good for this." I was too worked up and full to say anything. She tied my crossed hands to the bedposts and gave me a lashing with a buggy whip.

One day me and Little Mars' got into a fight. We had been playing, and all at once he hauled off and called me a name and hit me. He was much bigger than I was, but we tied up. He was getting the best of me, so I up and bit him on the jaw. I tried to pull a plug out of him. Oh, he hollered and squirmed, but I had him. I had awful big, stout teeth, and when I let go of him you could see the print of them in a circle on the jaw. Mars' Bill wasn't at home, so the mistress tied me and whipped me until she was tired. I was bloody all over. Then when the oldest boy came home and saw what I had done to Little Mars', his brother, he took me down to the barn and tied me across a wagon wheel and whipped me until I couldn't hardly move.

As soon as I was able to get up and walk a little, I had to go to the office to wait on Mars' Bill. He was a doctor, and I had to go and bring him water and hand him things while he was cutting on people and pulling teeth. I went in bloody and nasty. He said, "Charlie, what is the matter with you? What have you been doing?" I said, "Mistress whipped me." He said, "What for?" I said, "Nothing, Mars' Bill, she just whipped me because she wanted to." He got awful mad. When he came home that evening he called the mistress and said, "What did you whip that boy that way for?" She said, "The black devil bit his master's jaw." "Matters not if he did," said Mars' Bill. "You shouldn't have cut him up like you did. Here I was offered just seven hundred dollars for him yesterday, and the man will be here to look at him tomorrow, and what do you think the man will give me for him with his back all cut to pieces like it is?" They had an awful row, and he was mad enough to slap her. She pouted around and wouldn't eat nothing for days. I was awful sore on my back and legs. The women took feathers and kept me greased in castor oil to keep my shirt from sticking to the cuts.

I got another awful whipping about a year later from Ole Missey. This time it was for telling on her. Mars' Bill was always missing some of his money and getting after me about it. One morning before he got up I heard Ole Missey in the room stirring around, so I took a peep through the crack of the door to see what she was doing. I looked just in time to see her take two dollars out of Mars' Bill's pocket. Away by and by, he got up and put on his clothes and felt in his pocket. As soon as he missed the money, he called Ole Missey and said, "Did you take two dollars out of my pocket?" She said, "No, I didn't take it. That black devil of a Charlie about took it." He called me, "O Charlie, come here you rascal. You son of a bitch, did you take two dollars out of my pocket?" "No, sir, Mars' Bill. Ole Missey took your two dollars, for I saw her when she did it. I was looking through the crack of the door." She flew into flames. "You lie, you black devil. Don't you accuse me of stealing your master's money." Mars' Bill just stood right still for a minute. Then he turned to her and said, "Now just hush. Don't you say any more. I believe this boy is telling the truth because I can feel it." She got awful mad, and when Mars' Bill went out she came over to me and shook her fist in my face and said, "You black, ugly devil, as soon as your master leaves I am going to tear your back all to pieces."

Sure enough, as soon as Mars' Bill left she called me in. She was sitting in a big chair and had a heavy strap in her hand. "Come here and kneel down, you black devil. I am going to whip you half to death." She grabbed me by the back of the head and pulled it down between her knees. She had me there and commenced to working on me. In a few minutes I began to feel smotherified. She was holding my head so tight that I couldn't move, and her coattail was shutting all the air off. When a man feels his wind being cut off he will do about anything. I couldn't get my head out, so I just twisted sorter to one side and bit her on the leg. She let go of me mighty quick and just hollered.

When Mars' Bill got home that evening, she was sitting in the room sniffing and crying. He said, "What is the matter?" She said, "That black, ugly devil, Charlie, bit me." He got awful mad and red. He asked her how I come to bite her. When she told him, he changed colors and said, "Now, I have always told you never to whip any of these niggers that way. There is a good cowhide on the back porch and also a buggy whip, and whenever you want to whip any of them you can tie them to the crib and use those whips."

I thought he was going to give me another beating, but he gave me a hard slap in the face and told me to be gone.

Before the war I used to be waiting on the table. Sometimes I would be awfully hungry, but I wore a long white apron that came to my feet and couldn't take nothing off the tray. The apron went over my shoulders, around my waist, and buttoned behind down to my feet. One night we had some awful good biscuits for supper, and I wanted some of them so badly I didn't know what to do. I didn't get biscuits to eat, just corn bread and fat meat. The only biscuits I ever got were those I would sometimes take off the tray and gobble down between the kitchen and dining room. These particular biscuits were so large that I couldn't get one in my mouth, so I just grabbed off two and threw them down by a tree between the kitchen and dining room. (The kitchen was not connected with the big house.) But as I was going in the door old Bruno, my master's dog, ran up and ate them biscuits. I was so mad I didn't know what to do; but I had to go on in the house. When I got through passing around the table, I came out and took that wooden tray and threw it at old Bruno and busted the tray all to pieces against a tree stump. When I went back in the dining room they were all sitting around the table, waiting and watching for me to come in with the tray full of dessert. Ole Missey was very proud of me because I could step around a table. She used to boast a lot about me. I went in with one plate of dessert in each hand. I could see her face change the minute I stepped in the door. I started to the company with the plates. She looked up at me, her face as red as a beet, and said, "What does this mean, your coming in my dining room without a tray, sir?" Then my master took it up and asked me, "Where is that tray, you _____ _____, good-for-nothing rascal." I said, "I stumbled and fell and broke it." I didn't much care how I spoke, for I knew what was coming. If he had been going to kill me I would have said the same thing, because I just didn't care. I had neither mother nor father, and I had just as soon been dead as alive.

Me and my brother were awfully mischievous and had some times. We used to swipe chickens and roast them in the fire, guts and all. Then we would just rub our hands over them, and the skin would peel off. We would take turns about eating while the other watched.

Whenever we wanted a good chicken we would get up early in the morning and go to the henhouse. One of us would go in, and the other would go up to the big house to watch. We always carried a bucket and a few gravels in our hand. This was used to give warning. The one that was on watch would, if he saw any signs about the big house, drop a pebble in the bucket as a signal. We used the bucket so that, in case our master should catch us up so soon, we could tell him that we were going to the spring for water. We used to be up and about all the time. Whippings couldn't stop us.

My brother Jeff was the only kin I had that I knew anything about while I was coming up. We used to get off to ourselves at times and figure how we would some day run away. One night we were behind the corncrib, talking. We would meet there because Jeff was a field hand, and I always worked about the big house—cutting wood, waiting on the table, and making fires. Sometimes I had to wait on the sick, empty chambers, clean out the privy, and just do anything. So I didn't stay in the cabin where my brother stayed. That is why we used to meet behind the corncrib.

My brother had an awful heavy voice and couldn't talk low, so while we were talking our master came up and listened to what we were saying. I remember so well how I swore and said, "I'll be damned if I want to run away and be brought back here and whipped and then have to have my back greased in castor oil. When I run away I am going for good." About this time our master stepped around the corner of the crib and said, "You two damn rascals are plotting to run away, are you? Come right around here and I will teach you how to run away. I will tear your _____ and backs to pieces." Jeff jumped up and ran, but I went on around the crib to take my whipping. In the side of the crib was a hole, and whenever we got whipped we had to lean over and stick our heads through this hole. Our hands were crossed and tied and stuck through also. In a bent position like this, you know about where a man's shirttail would be.

Before he hit me a lick, Mars' Bill said, "Charlie, you rascal, what were you and Jeff around there plotting to run away for?" I said, "Mars' Bill, we were not plotting on how to run away." I said this because we were not plotting on how to run away. My brother was, but I wasn't. That don't sound like we was plotting, do it? I was, in fact, trying to get Jeff not to go. I knew he didn't have a chance to get away right at that time for so many had tried and been tracked by the bloodhounds and brought back and then beat mostly to death. So I wasn't lying when I said that we was not plotting. But he said, "You black son of a bitch, I will tear your _____ all to pieces." With this the strap began to crack. I twisted and squirmed about, but I didn't shed a tear. After giving me about ten lashes, he said, "Charlie, I am not whipping you for fixing to run away but because you told me a lie." He got mighty mad and hit me twenty more lashes. I said, "I thought you told me that if I told you the truth you wouldn't hit me another lick." "Shut up, you lying rascal; I'll fix you so you can't sit down and talk to anybody in peace." I guess he would have whipped me more, but he stopped all at once and said, "Where is that damn Jeff?" But Jeff had gone. My master left me in the stock and ran to the house to get the dogs. He let me loose and told some of the women to grease me from my neck to my heels. He woke up some of the men in the shacks, and they all went after Jeff. They caught him early the next morning and brought him back. I thought they would surely whip him to death. However, when they got back, Mars' Bill sent him on to work and kept strict watch over him and didn't hit him a lick. The first time I got close to Jeff he said, "Now you see what you get for being scared to run away. I started off and got caught, but he didn't whip me like he did you." I said, "Yes, but I'll bet he is going to give you a lashing sooner or later."

And sure enough, he did. There were three men and their wives come over on the following Sunday to take dinner with the white folks, and after dinner Mars' Bill rung the bell and had Jeff sent for. They took him to the crib, and they all went around him with straps. Ole Missey and the other white women that had come to see her was in the big house, looking out of the upstairs windows. The men stood between them and my brother Jeff so that they could see the blows but not see his naked back. They nearly whipped him to death, but it didn't take the starch out of him, for as soon as he got well and felt able he began to talk about going again. And he did go. But it was not until the war that he got away for good.

When the war started, Jeff run off and joined the Yankees over on the other side of Nashville. I stayed because I was yet young and didn't know so much about what it meant. Mars' Bill looked for him and went around cussing and saying what he was going to do to him when he caught him. But he never did catch him. Jeff was gone, and I sometimes cried because he was my only brother and I felt lonesome all the time.

One night when I was out getting some wood for the fire I heard somebody call me. He said, "Charlie, Charlie!" I said, "Who in the devil is that calling me?" He said, "For God's sake, Charlie, hush; don't talk too loud. Come here; I am Jeff." I said, "I don't believe it. I will take a piece of this stove wood and knock the devil out of you." He tried to make me hush because he was afraid of the dogs. Mars' Bill had four mighty bad dogs, and no doubt about it. If those two bitches and old Rover and Trixy got around you somebody would sure get bit. So Jeff slipped up behind the crib and tried to attract my attention by whispering.

He threw some green apples at me and said again, "Charlie, for God's sake, come here. I want to talk to you." By this time I recognized his voice and went where he was. He said, "Charlie, you are the only brother I have got, and I want you to come with me." I said, "Jeff, where in the name of the devil have you been, and where can we go?" He said, "I am with the Yankees, and I slipped off to come and get you. I have been ducking and dodging for three days trying to get here. I want to take you with me. Don't be scared of the Yankees. And even if we should get killed, it won't be much worse than staying here."

I was scared of the Yankees and especially the cavalry, for I had seen troops of horses go by and they looked so awful and sounded like thunder. Too, Mars' Bill had always told me that the Yankees were mean and would kill all the Negroes they could get their hands on. But after I heard what Jeff said I made up my mind to go. I was still young, less than twenty, I know. I said, "Jeff, you know there are some bad dogs here, and they can track you. Now I tell you what you do. You jump over the fence here, cross the creek, go over in the graveyard by the peach orchard, and wait for me." He said, "All right." And I went on back to the kitchen and got ready to take the suppers to the cabins for the field hands. As I left the kitchen with the victuals, I grabbed off a piece of corn bread and a slice of meat about the size of a man's hand and dropped them in a bucket right outside the kitchen door. I went on in the cabin, and while they were squabbling as they always did—each one trying to grab the biggest piece of bread and get most of the gravy—I went up in the loft and threw out what things I had up there. I also took along a piece of an old quilt. I came down from the loft and went back to the kitchen. I got the smokehouse key and went out and cut down half a shoulder of beef and a big piece of side ham. I would have taken more, but I was in a hurry. I put the meat in a sack and hid it. Then I went to the kitchen. I always worked around the house and kitchen, so the cook didn't pay me no attention. The first chance I got I took a big pan and filled it with meal and carried it out and poured it in the sack with the meat. I ran out then, bundled up everything, threw the sack across my shoulder, and left.

I found Jeff right where I told him to go. He said, "Charlie, what is in them bundles?" I said, "My clothes, and something to eat." I fished around in the meal and got out the piece of bread and meat I had dropped in there. He ate like a dog and said the meat was good because it had salt in it and he hadn't had any salt bacon in a long time.

We got up and started to walking and running until we both gave out. I guess it was about midnight when we stopped to rest. We were in a large, open pasture, so we looked around to find a place where we could kinder hide and sleep. Finally we came to a deep gully, and in it we jumped. I spreaded down the old piece of quilt and used my other little bundle for a pillow. We must have been awfully tired for we went to sleep right away, and the next morning when we woke up there was a great bunch of cattle standing over the ditch looking down on us. They had their heads low and their tails hoisted. I said, "Jeff, we had better get away from here, for if anybody should come along they would see the cows standing and come over to see what was the matter." We got up and left. About an hour later we came to a thick woodland —this was about six or eight miles out from Nashville. We sat down and began to talk about something to eat. I said, "I got some meal and meat, but how can we cook it?" Jeff said, "Charlie, you go find some water, and I will do the rest." I found a little spring not far away and came back and told him. He took his axe—he always carried his axe—and cut a big chip out of a tree. He made a fire, propped some meat up before it on a stick, and let the grease drip on the big chip. While this was going on he took some meal in his hat, went to the spring, and mixed up some bread. The big green chip was greasy and hot by this time, and Jeff just poured the batter on it and left it there before the fire.

While we were waiting, some Yankees came by on horses. All the men had their helmets tied under their chins, and the horses' hoofs sounded like thunder as they went running down the road. It nearly scared me to death, and I started to run, but

Jeff caught me and said, "Charlie, the Yankees won't hurt you. Haven't I been with them nearly a year? They are fighting Mars' Bill and the other white folks. They don't want to do nothing to us. They will pay us for our work, and if Mars' Bill tries to get us after we get among them he will get his foot into it. For they told me that I didn't have to ever go back to him unless I wanted to." Still, I kept feeling funny and nervous. But I guess it was due to the war. Nobody is like hisself during a war, I reckon.

The Yankees didn't see us, so I ate my bread and meat in peace. When we got through we went on our way. We met an old slave man way late that day. He was tired and hungry and he said he hadn't had anything to eat for three days. I believe it, for he almost cleaned us, and when he got full he tried to dissuade us from running away. He told us that Mars' Bill was our friend, and that we never had to want for anything. I was listening to him and so was Jeff, but all at once Jeff jumped up and said, "Oh, hell! Charlie, let's go; I know what is best for us. Let everybody else do like they want to do."

After we got some distance off I said, "Jeff, we had better run, because if Mars' Bill and the others should be after us they might see that old man, and he would tell them which way we went." I didn't let on that I was thinking this until we left, because Jeff was mighty fiery and might have got suspicious of the old man and done him dirt with his axe.

We got to the camp early the next morning, just as the Yankees were taking the Negroes out to work. There must have been about a thousand slaves, and they all had axes, going out to cut wood. One troop of cavalry went in front and another behind. This was to protect the slaves from the rebels. There was a lot of bushwhacking, for the two main armies were fighting just a few miles on the other side of Nashville.

When we came in sight of the advance horsemen, two of them came riding real fast toward us with pistols in their hands. I got scared and jumped behind a tree and wouldn't come out. They hollered to Jeff and said, "Halt, who goes there?" Jeff threw up his hands and said, "A workman of the camp, Number 89." By this time one of them was up on me. He said, "Who are you?" I said, "I am Charlie X." He said, "Whose slave are you?" I said, "I belong to Mars' Bill." "What do you want here then? Didn't your master treat you good?" I said, "Yes, Mars' Bill treated me all right, but I wanted to be free, and I came with my brother over here to work." All the others had come up about this time and, after talking a little while, they told me to fall in line with my brother and the rest of the workers.

I worked, cutting wood, until they commenced fighting near our camp. We didn't have much to eat at times, and often some of the troopers would take us out to round up two or three cows that had been taken by the Yankees and herded into certain places. We would kill a beef, cut off the head, take out the guts and insides, skin it, and cut the meat into big chunks. Then we would put our meat on a long, forked pole, one end buried in the ground and the other slanting up and pointing towards the fire. Just a little salt sprinkled on it, and it was left to cook before the fire. When the meat was done, such eating and smoking you never heard. It used to make me awful sick at times, and I would throw up a lot. But I was hungry, and kept trying until I made it stick in my stomach. When a man goes two or three days without eating, he has to be careful how he loads his stomach the first time, else he will surely get as sick as a dog.

After the fighting shifted over to where we were, we had to lay awful close. The cannonballs were coming over, cutting off treetops just like nothing. One night they called us all together and told us that if we wanted to be saved we would have to go to the river and get down in the hull of "Old Ironside." Such a scrambling to get there I never saw. They were just jamming and cramming in. I looked at it and said, "I can't live in there, and since I am going to die anyhow, I had rather die in the open." The shots and shells were flying like bees, but I slipped away and ran along the riverbank until I came to an old hollow tree. One side of it had been burnt out by lightning or something, and it was leaning over nearly to the ground and close to the river. I crawled up in there and hid. I thought I was safe, but just about the time I got settled a cannonball came over and cut off the top of a tree nearby, and the limb fell in the water under me and covered me with mud and slime. I said, "I had better get out of here." I had a hard time getting out, for the tree limbs had almost blocked up the place where I had crawled in. I got up and ran. I ran nearly all night, scared to death. Just before day I came to an old colored man's house. I took my axe and pried the door open, went in, took his gun, set it outside the door, and sat down before the fireplace. When he woke up and saw me he looked scared, but he jumped up and reached for his gun. Not finding it, he looked at me. I was now standing. He said, "Who are you, son?" I told him what had happened and asked him to let me stay with him until the storm [battle] was over. He consented, and we stayed together.

But we didn't have much to eat and there was no place to get anything. There wasn't no such a thing as a store to buy, even if they had had any money to buy with. Too, the battle was raging all around Nashville at that time. I began to pray mightily unto the Lord and said, "Save me, Lord! Save me!" I said, "If I stay here I will starve to death or get killed, so I might as well get further." I went down by the Cumberland River—the shells were booming and falling everywhere. I kept going, praying and running. I got to the river and found a canoe chained to a big rock. I unloosed the chain and got in and paddled across the river. I didn't have no paddles, so I just lay flat on my belly and paddled along with my hands. I didn't know where I was going; I just wanted to cross over on the other side.

It was nighttime, so when I got across everything was quiet. I started to walking along the bank. After a while I came to a rock fence. All at once somebody hollered, "Halt! Halt!" It sounded like a thousand voices had come all at once from one end of the wall to the other. These were guards. They slept on their arms, standing in their places. As soon as they saw me they all raised their guns, and after making me halt they told me to throw up my hands and advance. My heart was pumping in my bosom so I couldn't hardly stand or move.

I expected to be shot every minute. I said, "Save me, Lord! Oh, save me!" I advanced and found that they were bluecoats [Yankees]. They asked me where I was from and what I wanted there. I told them that I belonged to Mars' Bill, but that I had been working in the Yankee camp and got lost from the other workers when the battle started. They talked among themselves for a while and then told me to go to the rear. I went on back, halting nearly every minute until I got where there was a lot of other slaves in quarters. They were being used to dig trenches and throw up breastworks. The next day we went to work a good ways off. At first everything was quiet, but along towards dinner time, twelve o'clock, old General Hood had his men all scattered around in the woods for battle. When the Yankees on Capitol Hill gave the signal— God bless your soul—it sounded like the cannons would tear the world to pieces. I could hear the big shells humming as they came. They cut off treetops just like a man cutting off weeds with a scythe. Big shells and little ones. Some were chained together and what not. You could hear them hit the ground and then burst.

They didn't give us any orders as to what to do, so we started to running. They tried to make us keep on working by telling us that the rebels were beyond us and that the shells were aimed at them, but every time one came over I hollered, "O Lord, save me, save me!" That night we hid in the woods, every man for himself. I was running, stumbling, and falling. All the time I would call on the Lord.

Early next morning I came face to face with some Confederate soldiers, and who should be among them but a boy that had lived on the adjoining plantation to Mars' Bill's. He recognized me and said, "Charlie, what are you doing out here?" I told him I was lost. I thought they were going to kill me, but he said, "I won't let anybody hurt you, Charlie. How is Mama and my sisters?" I told him they were at home and well the last time I saw them. He looked so awful I told him this to cheer him up. His feet were sore and all swelled up, and his jaws were long. He looked almost like death. He said, "Charlie, damn if I am going to fight anymore; I haven't had anything to eat for days, and I am just fagged out."

There were some chickens down the hill a little ways. He said, "Charlie, catch me one of those chickens." I lit out after one of the chickens, and it rose and flew but it might as well have stayed on the ground. When I got back he said, "Now catch me one of them shoats there." I tore out down the hill after the old sow and the pigs. I legged one and brought it back. They took their knives and just slit him down the belly and let the guts fall out. Then they stuffed it and the chicken down in a bag and said, "Goodbye, Charlie, and good luck. We are going."

I wandered around in the woods, scared to death. I didn't know which way to go nor what to do. Along towards evening I came upon a group of Yankees. They halted me and asked me where I belonged. I said, "I belong to Mars' Bill." Then they asked me where Mars' Bill lived. I told them that he lived right across the river. They said, "What are you doing over here?" I said, "I have been working, cutting wood and building breastworks for the Yankees." One of them gave me a little piece of paper with some writing on it and told me to go about a mile and report to Captain K. I couldn't read, so I didn't know what the writing was. I had one mind not to go, but I kept going along slowly, wondering all the time what they would do to me. I was just nervous and scared. Times were so desperate along these days. All I did was to call on the Lord. "Lord, save me; save me, Lord!" He saved me, and that is why I trust in him today.

I went to Captain K., and he put me to work again. This time I stayed and was not in any more danger during the rest of the war. I never did hear from my brother, or about the boat in which all those people had hidden. I don't know whether the boat got sunk and all got drowned or not, but I thanked God for my spared life.

During slavery, and even after the war, the white people used to be awfully mean to the Jews and to the Irish. Sometimes the Irishmen used to slip around the cabins and fields and beg the slaves to keep them. They would say, "Mister, give me a little something to eat or help me along a little." Sometimes the slaves would help them, and sometimes they wouldn't. But whenever the masters would catch them on the plantation or around the cabins they would say, "What do you want here? Get off of this place." Then they would kick and cuff them and drive them off. All the Irish would do would be to say, "Oh, my Lord! Oh, my Lord!" and run away.

The Jews used to come around among us selling knives, razors, handkerchiefs, etc. The slaves usually had a little money because they saved every penny they got in order to raise one hundred dollars to pay for a run-away the first chance they got. Men used to cross to the North hauling big wagonloads of meat, and if any slave wanted to run away he would be hid in between the meat. When he got on the North side he paid the teamster or driver the one hundred dollars, and he could make his escape.

That is why the Jews always wanted to come among the slaves, because they usually managed to have a little money to buy pretty things. But if our masters ever caught them around, they would beat and kick them worse than they would the Irish. The Jews would say, "Oh mercy, God! Oh mercy, God!" and run away. The Jews have gone through some hard trials and tribulations but they are on top now, and the reason is that they have always had something to sell, and when they get a dollar they save it.

I remember after the war there were a lot of Jewish stores on or near Sixth and Grant Streets, and the people used to talk about how worrisome the Jews were whenever you passed along the street. They would stand on the front, and when anybody passed along they would grab him by the hand and say, "Come in, I want to sell you something. Come in and let me show you. I got good goods." I used to pass along there a lot, and I made up my mind to have some fun the first time one of them took hold of me. Sure enough, the following Saturday I was passing along, and one of them took hold of me and said, "Come in, I got a shirt that will just fit you." I said, "I don't want no shirt." He was still holding on to me, so I took hold of him and started running down the street. He just hollered, "Hey, let go! Let go! I got to go back to the store." I let go of him, but he kept on after me to come back and see some woolen shirts. I went and looked at them. They were not woolen shirts. I was sure of that as soon as I looked at them. I said, "These shirts are not woolen." He said, "Oh yes, yes, they are woolen. You must be thinking of my son, Ikie, on the corner. Now he sells the same goods, but it is no such goods as this." I laughed and left the store. It sounded funny to me, and I don't reckon he knew what he was saying. Jews certainly can sell though.

After the war I was turned loose without a cent. I started out looking for something to eat and for some place to stay. I went from place to place, but everywhere I went I found the people in bad shape from the effects of the war. At the end of three days' tramping about I came to a house where some white people lived. I knew they had dogs and guns, but I was hungry. I hadn't eaten anything for three days. I knew there was food there, so I hid around until night. While they were all sleeping I went up and, by means of a hole in the door, was able to cut the latchcord so as to get into the house. I went in and found them all sleeping. I took my knife and cut off a big chunk of meat and got some other things and went down to the spring and started to eating. I was so hungry that I just poked it in as fast as I could. But I was sorry afterward, for I got so sick I didn't know what to do. I vomited up everything I had eaten.

I know that family was worried and sore when they found out what had happened, but I couldn't help it. I was just hungry and had to have something to eat.

I left that spring and made my way to old man B. W.'s house. I told him that I was motherless and fatherless and asked him to take me in as a member of the family. I said, "If you will just take me in I will do any kind of work. I just want some place to call home and people to take the place of my parents." He consented to let me stay awhile, but he wouldn't adopt me into his family. I went to the spring and washed out the clothes I had on and washed my body some. My hair was long and shabby, but I couldn't help it.

Not long after I started to staying with him, an old white man, Mr. L., hired me to work for him. He agreed to pay me thirty cents a day. Now, although I was a grown man, I couldn't count money. At the end of a year I don't know how much I had saved up, but old man B. W., in some way, took the money for a wagon and team and some harness. After doing this he tried to get rid of me. He would give me a gun and tell me to go out and shoot some game, but he began to call me lazy and good-for-nothing and told me to leave. I cried because I felt so lonesome and blue. I said to him, "I will go. You call yourselves Christians and pray for the widows and orphans, but you don't do anything for them."

I left, and some time after I got work for the government. I used to do hauling and all kinds of work. One day, while I was down on the public square, I met my old master. I had not seen him for nearly thirty years. He said to me, "Charlie, do you remember me lacerating your back?" I said, "Yes, Mars'." "Have you forgiven me?" he asked. I said, "Yes, I have forgiven you." There were a lot of people gathering around because we were a little distance apart and talking loud. I was never scared of nobody, so when he asked me the next question, "How can you forgive me, Charlie?" I said, "Mars', when we whip dogs, we do it just because we own them. It is not because they done anything to be whipped for, but we just do it because we can. That is why you whipped me. I used to serve you, work for you, almost nurse you, and if anything had happened to you I would have fought for you, for I am a man among men. What is in me, though, is not in you. I used to drive you to church and peep through the door to see you all worship, but you ain't right yet, Marster. I love you as though you never hit me a lick, for the God I serve is a God of love, and I can't go to his kingdom with hate in my heart." He held out his hand to me and almost cried and said, "Charlie, come to see me and I will treat you nice. I am sorry for what I did." I said, "That's all right, Marster. I done left the past behind me." I had felt the power of God and tasted his love, and this had killed all the spirit of hate in my heart years before this happened. Whenever a man has been killed dead and made alive in Christ Jesus, he no longer feels like he did when he was a servant of the devil. Sin kills dead but the spirit of God makes alive. I didn't know that such a change could be made, for in my younger days I used to be a hellcat. All the bad fellows around Nashville stood back when I came around. I was a great boxer and even now, though I am eighty-four years old, my arms and chest are active, and I don't believe many boxers today could make a punching bag out of my head. I am sorter down in my knees and thighs, though.

I used to drink a lot of whiskey. One night I went out on the White Creek Pike. I just went because I felt my manhood and wanted to carouse a little. I stepped in old man R.'s place and bought a few drinks of whiskey. Pretty soon I began to feel kinder dizzy. There wasn't many people in the place, just a few lounging around the old, long bench in the back of the room. There was a woman in there. I didn't know her, but I decided that I would like to get acquainted with her. She was a good-looking brownskin sure as you are born.

I walked over in the corner where there was a fiddler. The lamplight was so dim that I couldn't see who he was, and I didn't care. I said, "Strike up a tune on that fiddle. I feel like shaking my foot tonight." I could cut the pigeonwing all right, and I knew it. There wasn't many that could beat me in my prime. Somebody in the corner said, "There ain't gonna be no dancing here tonight." I was feeling rough and ready, for I had just enough whiskey under my belt to key me up. I said, "I will dance in this _____ place tonight if I have to dance over some of your dead bodies. Strike up 'Yankee Doodle,' boys, on that fiddle, or I'll blow this damn house into splinters."

I said this as if I had a gun, but I didn't have a thing. I started walking towards the lamp to throw it, but before I could reach it, who should come out of the far corner of the room but Bad Frank. He was much bigger and taller than I was, and stronger too, and was known to be a bad man. I had heard of him, but I had never been in no trouble with him. He came at me with a switch blade knife nearly six inches long. Now I never was a coward, but he had me hemmed off from the door. I decided to battle him with my fist. I knew that if ever I got one blow in on him it would be goodbye Annabell, for I was a scientific boxer and didn't fear the best. He came at me with a half-grin, as he always did when he was mad, calling me all kinds of names as he came. He was on me before he got his knife open. It was a switch blade, but it didn't open quick enough. He made a jerk at it with his right hand—he was left-handed. As he did this I saw my only chance and took advantage of it. I sorter crouched like a tiger, leaped right under his arms, and landed two blows on his chin before he could say scat. He fell clear across the room in the other corner. By this time the room was in an uproar. I said, "Come on you _____, for I am ready to fight the whole house." There was a table on one side of the room. I kicked it over and this made a great noise. They thought I was going to do some shooting. One little red-eyed fellow, that had been asleep, woke up and jumped out of the window. I gave a wild whoop and grabbed the lamp from the bar and busted it against the wall. About this time I saw my chance to get out, and I broke and ran. When I let up running I was nearly to Broad Street. I had run nearly six miles. I laid low after this and didn't go back into that part of the country for a long time, for I knew that some of them would be laying for me.

I got into another mix-up down in the old Martin Brick. I was dancing with a girl named A. A fellow by the name of X. was stuck on her and had been in two or three fights about her. I danced with her twice and asked her to give me another certain dance which was to be a cakewalk. She said, "All right." But I noticed she looked kinder funny. She was a good dancer, and I was too. That is why I asked her to dance with me, so I could cut some figures.

When time came I saw her standing in the corner talking to a man. I walked over and asked her if she was ready. Before she could say anything, her man spoke up and said, "No, she is not ready. Do you think you are going to dance with my woman all night?" I wasn't feeling for no fight, so I said, "Excuse me, friend, I didn't know that was your woman." He must have been mighty sore, for he said, "You try to be cute anyhow. I will make you jump out of some of these windows." I didn't say anything else because I didn't know but that his gang was there.

Late in the night things commenced to get rowdy. Everybody was drinking and having a time. I didn't dance with A. anymore. In fact, I had forgotten what had happened in the early part of the night. While I was standing off to one side, she came over and started to talking to me and asked me why I had not danced with her anymore. I didn't say anything, because I saw there was going to be some trouble. Her man came over and caught her by the shoulder and gave her a slap that sent her to the other side of the room. I knew that he meant to start something with me next, and when he did I was ready for him. As soon as he hit her I reached down and picked up a green piece of stovewood and hit him right across the earlocks. Somebody hollered, "Charlie done killed X." I didn't know but that his gang might double up on me, so I decided to get out. I ran to a window and just took my hand and smashed the glass, sashes and all, and jumped out. I jumped right in a barrel. Everybody was hollering and scrambling, trying to get out of the house. I jumped out of the barrel and ran like a wildcat. I went away out on the Hydes Ferry Pike.

Speaking of the Hydes Ferry Pike reminds me of the time I got held up out there near the bridge. I had been to a revival meeting and was on my way back home. I noticed a man acting kinder funny just in front of me as I crossed the bridge. When I overtook him he was near a clump of bushes. He said, "Hey, where are you going?" I hadn't joined church yet, and I wasn't scared of anybody. I said, "I am going home. Where do you think I am going?" About this time two other fellows came out of the bushes. They were all white men. They said, "Get ready to give up your money." The moon was shining pretty bright. I heard the sound of somebody coming across the bridge on a horse. I looked up and said, "Hey, friend, come here; these men are going to do me up." He came over and said, "What does this mean? Straighten up, you _____s, or I'll set this pike on fire." He told me to jump up behind him. I did, and he spurred the mule, and we went away just flying. He was one more nervy Negro. He told me after we got down the road a piece that he didn't have a thing, and that he was just bluffing.

Along about this time I was doing a powerful lot of courting. I had been paying attention to M. on the White Creek Pike. She was a good-looking little black woman, and nearly all the boys around were stuck on her. One day I went to see her. It was on Sunday, and the old folks had gone to church. I was feeling ambitious and devilish. I tried to talk to her and play, but she acted kinder queer and wouldn't have much to say. I asked her, "M., don't you love me? I thought you told me I was the best man." She said, "Charlie, sometimes I think I love you and then again sometimes I don't know." This put me on my p's and q's. You know how a young fellow is when he is about to lose something. He gets more careful. I said, "M., I am going away (it was in August) and won't be back no more until Christmas, and when I get back I am going to marry you." Sure enough I went down in Wilson County and didn't come back till Christmas. I got back with about thirty dollars in my pocket and a brand new suit of clothes. I went straight to see her. But when I got there, she was rocking a baby. I said, "Whose baby is that, M.?" She said, "Mine." I said, "I didn't leave no baby here when I left." She just hung her head and started to crying. I felt sorry for her and said, "That's all right, M., I am going away again, and when I come back next Christmas we will marry." This cheered her up. She said, "All right, Charlie; I will be waiting for you." But when I got back next Christmas she had another baby. I said, "Oh no, M., this won't do. One was bad enough, but two of them is too much to start out with." I didn't bother around her anymore.

I stayed around then and started to paying attention to another woman who was the daughter of the woman I boarded with. Now she had been married and had two children, but she was separated from her husband. I was very fond of sweet-potato custards, and she would make me one and just sit and watch me eat and put her arms around my neck and say, "Charlie, don't you love me better than you do Sis L.'s daughter?" I would tell her a lie and say, "Yes." But I gradually commenced to wean off from her. I liked her but she had two children, and too, she had been married once, and

I didn't care about starting out with a load at the beginning. I kept giving more and more attention to another woman, S., until I finally married her. She was as pretty as a speckled pup under a red running gear wagon. We knocked along for some time, but she was slow about giving me her hand. I finally got her, though, and it happened in this way. But first let me tell of my conversion.

When I first felt the power of God, I was in the woods. I had been feeling heavy and wanted to be converted. I went into the woods and said, "Lord, have mercy on me. I have been a sinner all my days." I got up and went home. The next morning, Sunday, I was boxing with R., who had come over with three or four others to swap a few with me. I was given up to be the best boxer around, and I laid them cold as fast as they came at me. While we were boxing a preacher by the name of Shelborne came by and called to me to come on to the revival, for he had a special seat for me. I told him I would come. I went, and he gave me a front seat. There I sat, night after night, for four days. On the fourth night, before going to church, I went into the woods and prayed again, saying, "Lord, I have neither father nor mother. Have mercy on me."

I went on to church, and the brothers and sisters prayed around me. Then, like a flash, the power of God struck me. It seemed like something struck me in the top of my head and then went on out through the toes of my feet. I jumped, or rather, fell back against the back of the seat. I lay on the floor of the church. A voice said to me, "You are no longer a sinner. Go and tell the world what I have done for you. If you are ashamed of me, I will be ashamed of you before my father." I looked about me and saw a deep pit that seemed to be bottomless. I couldn't hear nobody pray. I began to pray for myself. Again the voice said to me, "Go tell the world what great things the Lord has done for you." I rose from the floor shouting; a voice on the inside cried, "Mercy! Lord, have mercy!" It was about daybreak, and the two deacons that had stayed with me took me out of the church and left me. I ran to an elm tree nearby and tried to put my arms around it. Never had I felt such a love before. It just looked like I loved everything and everybody. I went to work that day shouting and happy.

There were two dogs at the house where I worked, and they were very dangerous, so much so that anyone coming up to the house had to be guarded by the family. I had always called at the gate and waited for some of them to come out and chain the dogs, but on this day I walked into the yard right by them neither trembling nor afraid. Neither of them did a thing to me. When God begins to work on the main altar of a man's heart, he don't have no time to fear or any thoughts of danger. Then a voice said, "When they ask you what is the matter, tell them what things the Lord has done for you." I went in the house and found them all there, and I began to shout. I was so glad. I felt so happy, and a love such as I had never felt before was welling up in my heart. Never since that day have I had any fear.

I can't tell you what religion is, only that it is love. If I do anybody wrong I feel grieved, get down on my knees, and ask for forgiveness from them. When the spirit struck me it seemed to hit me in the top of the head and go out through my feet. There is no such thing as getting religion, for it is love and a gift from God.

After the Lord turned me around, I began to feel that I needed a wife. One night I said to the Lord, "Lord, I need a helpmate. Direct me to a woman who will make me a wife." I knew when I prayed that the Lord would help me, but that I would, nevertheless, have to go and find the woman I wanted. My heart was set on S., and after I prayed this prayer I thought of her more than ever. And I decided she was the only woman for me.

However, I was boarding with a woman, and I kinder liked her daughter. One evening I dropped in—I didn't stay there every day—and was sitting down talking to Sister Y. Away after a while she turned to her daughter and said, "X., fix Brother Charlie some victuals. I expect he is hungry." I was awful hungry. All the time I was watching X., because I wanted to see how the spirit would move me towards her. She got up and just poked around and dragged about. While

I was waiting, I said, "Lord, I know this ain't the woman for me, for some day I might come in hungry, and if she was this slow I might forget myself, grab up something, and hit her with it. She was a good cook, but she just moved too slow to suit my taste.

Then I went to S.'s house. I liked her very much, but her folks didn't want her to have me. They thought I was a little too common, I reckon. Anyway they wouldn't let me see her much. On the day I went there and saw her turn about, I made up my mind that she was the woman I was looking for. When I went in and sat down her mother said, "Go fix Brother Charlie something to eat; he looks kinder hungry." No sooner had she spoked than S. jumped up and put the skillet on the fire; threw in two big slices of shoulder meat; set the coffee, put it on, and in no time she had the victuals on the table. All the time she was going about I was saying, "Lord, help me! Lord, help me!" She said, after she put the meal on the table, "Come on, Brother Charlie, the supper is ready." I turned around to the table, but I didn't eat a bite. I was just looking at her. She said, "You are not eating. I thought you were hungry." I said, "The sight of you would fill any man, unless his heart was of stone."

I sat there at that table and talked to her until the chickens started crowing for day. I grabbed my hat and ran over three miles to work. I hadn't eaten a bite. My heart was just jumping in my bosom. I plowed, sang, and prayed all day long, and when night came I wasn't tired a bit. I knew then that I had found my mate. But I had a time getting her.

One day I was plowing for a Mr. L. I was getting a dollar and thirty cents a day. A friend of mine came out in the field and said, "Oh, yes, Charlie, your beloved has gone to town today." I said, "Whoa mule! How long has S. been gone?" He said, "About two hours." I took out the team and started to the barn. Mr. L. said, "Charlie, if you quit work you can't come back." I said, "Mr. L., I got this job and I can get another one." I went to the barn, put up the horses, went to my shack, washed my face, feet, and under my arms, and put on my jeans pants and rolled them up nearly to my knees. I took my hat in my hand and my coat on my shoulder and hit the pike.

I must have walked some, for I met them as they were coming up Capitol Hill. I walked up to the express and said, "Have you sold out?" They had brought in a big load of butter, eggs, milk, and chickens. I said to S., "What do you think about marrying? I have come to give you up or to take you. I need you in my business." She said, "I haven't thought, and I don't think I will." I noticed the girl sitting on the seat beside her was pulling her dress and telling her to say no. I said, "Get down and come over here and let me talk to you." When she came over I said, "S., I love you. Are you willing to take me as a husband? If we don't marry today we don't marry at all." She looked straight at me but said nothing. I said, "Come on, we will go get the license." I rolled down my pants, put on my coat, and went over to the courthouse to get the license.

When we went in, the man was sitting with his feet propped up on the desk. He didn't look around so I said, "I want to get some license." He turned around but didn't get up and said, "What kind of license do you want?" This made me kinder mad. I wasn't in none too good a humor anyway. I said, "Now if I had been Mr. Gould or some other big man coming in here, you wouldn't have sat back that way and asked what kind of license do you want. You would have been up before I got in the door good. I want some marriage license." He said, "All right, I will get one for you." I took the license, and we went on and married. But I didn't go home with her. I went out on the White Creek Pike to the other woman's house, and she fixed me some good victuals that night. She asked me, "Charlie, are you going to marry Sis L.'s daughter?" I said, "No, not while I live." But I had already married her. The next day she found it out and asked me why I had treated her so bad. I just told her that it was easier to take care of two than it was to take care of four. She got sick and stayed sick a long time. I stayed with my wife forty years and never hit her a lick or even made her cry by speaking roughly.

After the war everything was tore all to pieces. Nobody had anything. I went from pillar to post, looking for work and something to eat. I didn't have any kin in the world that I know of. I got a job on Mr. X.'s farm for forty cents a day. I had to be up and have my team fed and ready for the field by four o'clock. Then I plowed until sundown. I was ambitious and wanted to have something, so I saved my money, and it wasn't long before I was able to buy a team of my own. I don't know how old I was when I married, but I looked the matter through and took the proposition to the Lord, and he led me to the woman that I married and cherished, forsaking all others until she died four or five years ago.

We had some pretty hard times after we first married. Times were hard and money scarce. Our four children were born three years after we married, so I had to go about mighty to provide for them and my old lady. I moved on a farm owned by old Bishop R. and stayed on and sharecropped, giving him one third. One day he came by my little shack in his buggy and said, "Charlie, I want your woman to come up to the big house and do some work for my wife." I said, "What woman?" He said, "S., your wife, of course." I said, "I tell you, Bishop, when I married my wife I married her to wait on me, and she has got all she can do right here for me and the children." He got awful mad and said, "Well, Charlie, I keep this house for people who can do what I want done. It is the custom for whoever lives here to let his wife help around the big house, and if you can't let your wife do it, I need my house." He tried to make me move right away, but I went to court, and they made him let me stay on until I got well.

That fall we moved into town, Nashville. I was still sick, so my wife got a job at the Union Stockyard up on Jo Johnston Street. They paid her twenty-two and a half cents a day, and this is what we had to live off of. One day before she started to work we didn't have anything to eat, or any fire, and it was cold. I knelt down and prayed. Then I got up, hobbled around and got my clothes on, and went up to the office. A certain Mr. O. and a lot of men were sitting around talking business. I opened the door and walked in. I took off my hat and looked them square in the eye. When a man gets hungry he is bold. I said, "Gentlemen, I am an ex-slave. I was loyal to my master, and as a free man I want to be a man and not a burden on my neighbors. But I am not able to work, and my wife and children are at home hungry and without food or fire." Then, still looking them straight in the eye, I said, "Will you help me, gentlemen? Will you help me?" Mr. O. asked me where I lived. Then he got up and spoke to the rest of them. He sent me home, and that evening they sent me enough food and fuel to last me a month.

When my wife started to work there she would bring home a little something to eat at night and a little fuel, and this is what we lived off of until I got well.

After I got well I got a job at the brickyard for a dollar a day. With this money I bought this property. I had to scuffle about mightily, but I got it paid for. I worked hard all the time. If I got out of a job at one place, I would look for one somewhere else. Once I got a job helping a certain man with his crops. He used to pay everybody off in their hats. One day he came out and put my money in my hat and said, "Here is your money, Charlie." I looked in the hat and found that he hadn't paid me enough. I said, "This money ain't right. I am due more money than this." He disputed me and said it was right. I said, "You are going to pay me my money." With this I walked over, reached in his hat, and took out a handful of money and paid myself. He jumped up and said, "You are going to take my money, are you?" His brother spoke up then and said, "Pay the nigger and kill him." He left for the house to get his gun, I guess, but while he was gone I left. I had my money, so there wasn't no use to stay around to get into trouble. I never did see him anymore.

I worked for another man once, and he tried to beat me out of some money. I had been cleaning some brick for him, and when it came time to settle up, he didn't want to keep his contract. He even said he wasn't going to pay me. I told him I would knock every tooth he had down his throat. He grumbled around, but he paid every cent.

Along about this time I wasn't so well, but I didn't want to stop work on account of wanting to build me a house. We just had a little two-room shack. But I finally got too weak to work. I was all down in my back. When I got able, some of my friends told me to go to the infirmary on Broad Street and let Dr. X. operate on me. Since I didn't seem to be getting any better, I thought I would go. I dressed one day and walked down to see him. He examined me and said that I needed an operation, but that he would have to do it on a sunshiny day. He gave me a quarter and told me to take a wagon to the square and then take the car home. Cars in those days were pulled by mules. But I wanted to save the quarter, so I walked home. Just as I turned off of Jo Johnston Street to go home, somebody met me and told me my house had burned. I hurried on, and when I got home I found nearly everything I had burned up. I had some valuable papers and notes there. I had just sold a horse, and I knew I would have trouble to finish collecting on him with all my receipts and papers gone. I did have trouble, for the horse died and the man didn't want to finish paying for him. But I put the matter in the hands of the sheriff. He collected the money and paid it to me one day up on the square. The man was awful cut up and sore about it and shook his fingers in my face and said he would get me. It was nearly ten years before I ever saw him again.

One day I passed by his house—he lived about eight miles up the White Creek Pike. I had forgotten all about the matter, else I wouldn't have gone that way. He was sitting on his porch with his feet propped up on the banisters. As soon as he saw me he jumped up and went in the house right quick. Like a flash, the thought came to me who he was. I was a good runner, so I took out down the road, cut across a woodland, and came out on top of a hill. I looked back and saw him cutting across a field on his horse, thinking that he would head me off down the road a piece; but I was gone. He was a mean man. I guess he would have killed me if he could have caught me, and nobody would have ever known the difference. I would have just rotted out there in them hills.

When my house burnt down I didn't know what to do. I took my troubles to one who never fails me. I said, "Lord, I am shelterless and without money. Provide a way for me." Like a flash, the idea struck me—to call on my neighbors and friends to help me. Whenever the spirit strikes a man he moves and moves without fear or shame. I went around among my neighbors and brothers and said, "You all see what a fix I am in. Come on and help me. I need a house and haven't got the money to build. Come on and help me." Everyone that I asked came and lent a hand, putting in what time they could spare. Some brought nails, some hammers, saws, and pieces of lumber. We had a house built in no time. We got a little piece of furniture wherever we could until we could get along.

I couldn't make much money working, so I put out some fruit trees and grapevines. I used to grow some mighty fine peaches, but the trifling boys around troubled me all the time. Nearly every time I would go through the orchard there would be two or three up the trees and crawling around the fence. I would rock them out sometimes, and at other times I would catch them and tell them it was wrong to take other people's things.

One night I was sitting on the porch, and I saw somebody moving along under the trees. I picked up a rock and sent it whistling through a treetop. I didn't know anybody was up in the tree, but when that rock went through a man fell out like a beef. He jumped up and they both started to run, but I told them to stop or I would kill both of them. I went out and found that they were two white men. The one that fell out of the tree said, "Uncle, you like to hit me when you throwed up that tree." I said, "I meant to hit you, and if you don't get out of here, I will hit you sure enough."

I was glad when the trees stopped bearing. I cleared off the lot and started to raising Irish potatoes. I cleared as much as ten to fifteen dollars on each crop. Early in the morning I used to get up, take my wheelbarrow, and roll a barrel of potatoes up to Jo Johnston Street so as to get them hauled to the market. I kept watch on the market, so as to dig and sell to the best advantage. So by working hard and saving everything I could rake and scrape together, I got my property and paid for my house so I could live in it.

I learned to save through the advice of a white man who used to sell groceries and whiskey. I used to drive a wagon, and some days I would get awful cold. I would stop by his place and buy a little drink. One day I was so cold I went by his place a second time for a drink. I said, "Give me another drink, Mr. X. I am cold." He looked at me and said, "Charlie, you ought to save your money. Look at me, when I started in this place I didn't have nothing, but now I own this place and two or three others. I am in a house and you are out of doors. It is not how much you make, but what you save that counts." I went home and told my wife about it. I said, "S., we must try to save something. You are working for twenty-two and a half cents a day, and I am making a dollar a day. With what little food you bring from the stockyard restaurant we can feed the two children." We started out doing this and put a dollar, two dollars, then three dollars a week in the bank. It wasn't long before we had a good little saving.

Not very far from our house was a lumberyard, and that belonged to Mr. R. When it would rain hard a lot of the lumber used to get washed down the hill and on out to the Cumberland. I noticed this and hit upon a scheme to get some of it. I took some long poles and built a sort of gap across the little creek, and when it rained and washed the lumber down I could catch it.

One day Mr. R. came by and said, "Hey! Where did you get all of my lumber?" I said, "I caught it out of the creek." He said it belonged to him and that he wanted it. I told him that I had built a trap to catch the lumber, and I went nearly to the Cumberland River and got some of it. "It was washed away. How do you say it is your lumber?" He didn't like it, but he saw that I was right, so he let it drop. I used it to put two other rooms on my house. I am now living in it. I gave a man four dollars to help me build it.

We got along very well from this time on until my wife got cross and fussy. I used to be awful strict about her having beer around the house where the children were. Whenever I happened home after work and smelt beer I would get after her about it. I never hit her, but just talked to her and tried to show her how it might cause the children to start the habit. After so long a time she got tired of my strictness. One day I came home, and she had packed up her things and told me she was going away to live with her sister and people in St. Louis. I said, "S., there is no need for you to leave me. We are getting along pretty well. If you go to St. Louis you won't be able to take care of yourself, and your people will soon get tired of you. Why don't you stay here so we can raise the children like they ought to be raised. Don't you remember the sacred vow you took when we first joined hands in wedlock?"

In spite of all I could say and do, she went away. She stayed about twelve months and then came back to me. But it wasn't long before she left again. I told her she would be wishing for me and home, and sure enough she did. For she got sick, and her people put her off in a little old house to herself, with nobody to look after her. She got somebody to write me to come to her. I thought over it a long time before I made up my mind to go. I had money for I had been working, and too, I had a good garden and had sold eight or ten barrels of potatoes and nearly as many turnip greens.

I fixed up and went to her in St. Louis. When I got there I inquired about until I found her. The door was cracked open just a little. I walked up and knocked on the door and at the same time I pushed it open and went in. She looked at me and said, "Howdy, Charlie." I said, "Yes, here you lay. It is just what I told you. Your people didn't want to be bothered with you, and you are just laying here ready to die. I tried to get you to stay at home, but no, you had to come here, telling the neighbors around I was too strict when I was just telling you what was best." She said, "Oh, Charlie! Oh, Charlie, don't rebuke me that way. I don't think I am going to live much longer." She commenced to crying. This softened my heart, and I spoke more tender to her. I remembered my marriage vow to nourish and cherish her so long as life should last. I knelt down by the bedside and took her hand

and said, "S., I will stay with you until the last. You are the one and only woman I have ever loved." I went out and found a woman to stay with her and wait on her. I gave her a dollar a day.

I got out and started to looking for work, praying all the time for the Lord to help me and strengthen me in my condition. He heard my prayers, for I found a job and went right to work.

About a month after I got there, S. died. I had just said to her, "S., how do you feel?" She said, "Charlie, I won't be with you much longer." Just as she spoke she gave a leap and jumped out of the bed on the floor and died. She was awfully fat. She weighed about 275 pounds. So I went and got some of the men in the neighborhood to come and help me get her back on the bed. I was awfully sad and lonesome. I grieved about her a long time, but I went to a Friend who has never failed me and he comforted me and gave me hope. I had always been true to her. She used to come up on the square to the market every Saturday night and bring the children, and I would give her every cent I had made, and then she would give me back a quarter or fifty cents, whatever she wanted me to have for pocket change. We would buy our groceries and a little candy and sweetened water for the children and go home.

Once a woman met me on the street and offered to sell me her body for a little money to buy her something to eat. I didn't have but a dime, but I gave it to her and told her that I had a wife and two children and had too much respect for them to wallow in the mud. I told her she ought to try to make a living in a better way than that. I tried to live in the sight of God like I expect to meet him, for he sees all we do and hears all we say. He is writing down the time.

I stayed in East St. Louis for twenty years, and during that time I did not touch a woman. Once I went to a certain place to rent a room. I had told the lady I was coming, so she fixed up a room for me. I went in that evening and talked things over, but it was too pent up for me. I said to her, "I got in here all right, but how can I get out? I like to kinder see my way out of a place, so I can get some air in case it should get too hot for me in here. Whenever you try to cut off my air and freedom to move about you will always have trouble with me." At the back of the house she had a high, close fence. This, she said, was in order that the roomers could bring their friends in and slip out without being seen. I asked her if that was the kind of business she was engaged in. I paid her the week's rent of twenty-five cents and left.

I worked pretty hard all the time I was there. The first job I got was in a fertilizing plant, but not long after I started to working there I got hurt and had to go to the hospital and stay thirty days. I didn't like the job so much nohow; it always stunk so hard it almost made me sick.

After this I got a job in a lumberyard. I used to, while working, get happy and shout. I don't know why, but it looked like the spirit would begin to move on the inside, and I just couldn't hold my peace. I shouted, sang, and cried. I got along well.

I worked at a bran plant for a long time, trucking bran. I was the only man that had ever held this job without burning out. They had some of the swiftest men there I ever saw. Some of them would make three stitches on the mouth of a bran sack, and it would be sewed up for moving. I was a good man at trucking and keeping the bags moved as fast as they sewed them, but I saw that I was worth more money. So I went to Mr. F. and said, "Mr. F., I want more money. I am doing two men's work, and I don't loaf on your job, and I am the only man that can hold down my job without help." He looked at me funny and after a while he said, "I will raise you to three dollars a day." I said, "Make it three-fifty, Mr. F. I am a good man. It won't be anything to you; I am making the company money." All this time I was looking him squarely in the eye. He hung his head for a while and said, "Well, Charlie, I will give you three-fifty if you think you can hold that job down." I went back to work, and you talk about snatching sacks, I snatched them. I used to get happy and shout and Mr. F. wouldn't say anything. It didn't matter how long I talked, shouted, and cried. He would just say, "You-all let the preacher have his way."

I went to a Presbyterian church once, a white church. I was the only colored man there. After the sermon, the preacher called for those who felt that he had preached the word to come forward. A man and a woman jumped up almost at the same time and started to shouting and clapping their hands and saying, "Yes, I know I got a religion, for it is all in my bones." They had so much fire in them that my soul caught on fire, and I jumped too. Some said, "Look at that Negro going up." But I didn't pay them no attention. I went on, and the preacher reached out his hand and welcomed me. Whenever the spirit begins to play on the main altar of your heart, you will cry out no matter where you are or what people say.

god
struck
me
dead

I have always been a sheep. I was never a goat. I was created and cut out and born in the world for heaven. Even before God freed my soul and told me to go, I never was hell-scared. I just never did feel that my soul was made to burn in hell.

God started on me when I wasn't but ten years old. I was sick with the fever, and he called me and said, "You are ten years old." I didn't know how old I was, but later on I asked my older sister and she told me that I was ten years old when I had the fever.

As I grew up I used to frolic a lot and was considered a good dancer, but I never took much interest in such things. I just went many times to please my friends and, later on, my husband. What I loved more than all else was to go to church.

I used to pray then. I pray now and just tell God to take me and do his will, for he knows the every secret of my heart. He knows what we stand most in need of before we ask for it, and if we trust him, he will give us what we ought to have in due season. Some people pray and call on God as if they think he is ignorant of their needs or else asleep. But God is a time-God. I know this, for he told me so. I remember one morning I was on my way home with a bundle of clothes to wash—it was after my husband had died—and I felt awfully burdened down, and so I commenced to talk to God. It looked like I was having such a hard time. Everybody seemed to be getting along well but poor me. I told him so. I said, "Lord, it looks like you come to everybody's house but mine. I never bother my neighbors or cause any disturbance. I have lived as it is becoming a poor widow woman to live and yet, Lord, it looks like I have a harder time than anybody." When I said this, something told me to turn around and look. I put my bundle down and looked towards the east part of the world. A voice spoke to me as plain as day, but it was inward and said, "I am a time-God working after the counsel of my own will. In due time I will bring all things to you. Remember and cause your heart to sing."

When God struck me dead with his power I was living on Fourteenth Avenue. It was the year of the Centennial. I was in my house alone, and I declare unto you, when his power struck me I died. I fell out on the floor flat on my back. I could neither speak nor move, for my tongue stuck to the roof of my mouth; my jaws were locked and my limbs were stiff.

In my vision I saw hell and the devil. I was crawling along a high brick wall, it seems, and it looked like I would fall into a dark, roaring pit. I looked away to the east and saw Jesus. He called to me and said, "Arise and follow me." He was standing in snow—the prettiest, whitest snow I have ever seen. I said, "Lord, I can't go, for that snow is too deep and cold." He commanded me the third time before I would go. I stepped out in it and it didn't seem a bit cold, nor did my feet sink into it. We traveled on east in a little, narrow path and came to something that looked like a grape-arbor, and the snow was hanging down like icicles. But it was so pretty and white that it didn't look like snow. He told me to take some of it and eat, but I said, "Lord, it is too cold." He commanded me three times before I would eat any of it. I took some and tasted it, and it was the best-tasting snow I ever put into my mouth.

The Father, the Son, and the Holy Ghost led me on to glory. I saw God sitting in a big armchair. Everything seemed to be made of white stones and pearls. God didn't seem to pay me any attention. He just sat looking into space. I saw the Lamb's book of life and my name written in it. A voice spoke to me and said, "Whosoever my son sets free is free indeed. I give you a through ticket from hell to heaven. Go into yonder world and be not afraid, neither be dismayed, for you are an elect child and ready for the fold." But when he commanded me to go, I was stubborn and didn't want to leave. He said, "My little one, I have commanded you and you shall obey."

I saw, while I was still in the spirit, myself going to my neighbors and to the church, telling them what God had done for me. When I came to this world I arose shouting and went carrying the good news. I didn't do like the Lord told me, though, for I was still in doubt and wanted to make sure. Because of my disobedience, he threw a great affliction on me. I got awfully sick, and my limbs were all swollen so that I could hardly walk. I began to have more faith then and put more trust in God. He put this affliction on me because it was hard for me to believe. But I just didn't want to be a hypocrite and go around hollering, not knowing what I was talking and shouting about. I told God this in my prayer, and he answered me saying, "My little one, my grace is sufficient. Behold! I have commanded you to go, and you shall go."

When I was ready to be baptized I asked God to do two things. It had been raining for days, and on the morning of my baptism it was still raining. I said, "Lord, if you are satisfied with me and pleased with what I have told the people, cause the sun to shine this evening when I go to the river." Bless your soul, when we went to the river, it looked like I had never seen the sun shine as bright. It stayed out about two hours, and then the sky clouded up again and rained some more.

The other thing I asked God was that I might feel the spirit when I went down to the river. And I declare unto you, my soul caught on fire the minute I stepped in the carriage to go to the river. I had been hobbling around on a stick, but I threw it away and forgot that I was ever a cripple.

Later the misery came back, and I asked God to heal me. The spirit directed me to get some peach-tree leaves and beat them up and put them about my limbs. I did this, and in a day or two that swelling left me, and I haven't been bothered since. More than this, I don't remember ever paying out but three dollars for doctor's bills in my life for myself, my children, or my grandchildren. Doctor Jesus tells me what to do.

split
open
from head
to foot

When I was very small my people thought I was going to die. Mama used to tell my sister that I was puny and that she didn't think that she would be able to raise me. I used to dream nearly all the time and see all kinds of wild-looking animals. I would nearly always get scared and nervous.

I got sick and an old white doctor came to see me, and after he had looked at me and examined me, he turned and told my mother that I was sin-sick. I never did forget this.

I married when I was young, and my husband aggravated and worried me all the time. He used to tell me, "There ain't no use for you to keep on praying and pouting around like that all the time." He told me to meet him at a picnic one day so that we could dance. Before this I had promised my father on his deathbed that I wouldn't dance no more. He said to me, "Pray to God, daughter, so that we can be candidates together in heaven." I went on to the picnic and danced against my will.

Some time later I got heavy one day and began to die. For days I couldn't eat, couldn't sleep; even the water I drank seemed to swell in my mouth. A voice said to me one day, "Nora, you haven't done what you promised." And again it said, "You saw the sun rise, but you shall die before it goes down." I began to pray. I was making up my bed. A light seemed to come down from heaven, and it looked like it just split me open from my head to my feet. A voice said to me, "Ye are freed and free indeed. My son set you free. Behold, I give you everlasting life."

During all this time I was just dumb. I couldn't speak or move. I heard a moaning sound, and a voice said, "Follow me, my little one, and I will show you the marvelous works of God." I got up, it seems, and started to traveling. I was not my natural self but a little angel. We went and came to a sea of glass, and it was mingled with fire. I opened my mouth and began to pray, "Lord, I will perish in there." Then I saw a path that led through the fire. I journeyed in this path and came to a green pasture where there were a lot of sheep. They were all of the same size and bleated in a mournful tone. A voice spoke to me, and it sounded like a roar of thunder: "Ye are my workmanship and the creation of my hand. I will drive all fears away. Go, and I go with you. You have a deed to your name, and you shall never perish."

you must die this day

When the voice first spoke to me I was in the cotton patch; I had just stopped dancing. A voice that seemed on the inside said, "Be still, my little one. You must die this day." Inside me, something was saying, "Mercy! Mercy!" I said to myself, "That is some dead person talking to me."

As I got to the big road I was a big-headed beast. The voice said again, "You must die." I said, "If I die I sure must go to hell." I went home and took my baby in my arms. The voice inside cried, "Mercy! Mercy, Lord!" I laid the baby down, for I thought the child was talking. A voice said, "You must die." I left home and went into the thicket and fell down, crying unto the Lord. There the power of God struck me, and a little man appeared and said, "My little one, follow me." Then, as quick as a flash, little Mary came out of old Mary, and I stood looking down on old Mary lying at hell's dark door. I saw the people in hell, and they were rolling over and over and crying, "Got no time; got no time." I traveled on east.

I journeyed with my little child, Hannah. As I went on I saw a well, and there was an old man. I went to him and asked for a drink of water. He turned, clapped his hand, and said, "Hi"—calling a pack of dogs. They ran me towards the north. I saw a level plain and a lot of long-horned cows. They blew at me. I was trying to get to an old house when I saw the cows and the dogs behind me. I was afraid, and as I looked up I saw a man coming from the north in midair, and he said, "Go on, for I will suffer no hurt nor harm to come to you." I went on and came to a high fence, and I cried, "Lord, how can I get out of here?" The voice said, "Go on; I will suffer no hurt nor harm to come to you." I looked to the east and there, nearby, was a little white path. I followed this and came to the top of the hill. It was so pretty and level. I looked to the east and saw a beautiful field with golden wheat and sheep there, eating. I looked to the south and saw a beautiful green pasture, and the sheep there were grazing. They turned their heads in the same direction and continued eating and began to bleat, saying, "Mama! Mama!" Then a voice on the inside answered me in the same tone.

Since that day I have been traveling, trusting in the Lord. Through the spirit I have come to see the meaning of the thicket briars, the snakes, the dogs, and the cows. They were my enemies.

fly open for my bride

God first spoke to me when I was eight years old. I was down in the thicket, getting some brush to kindle a fire. A voice called from I don't know where, saying, "O ye generation of vipers! Who had warned you to flee from the wrath to come? My little one, you are now eight years old. Go and ask the Lord to have mercy on your dying soul." I was so scared that I couldn't move. Finally I came to myself and ran home to tell Mama what I had heard. She told me to pray and said, "Daughter, it is true that you are eight years old." From this time on, I went often to the peach orchard and prayed. One day while praying—I don't know what I was saying more than "Lord, have mercy"—a voice spoke to me saying, "Go tell the world I have freed your soul." I was only nine years old at the time.

But I didn't tell anybody, because I was ashamed and I didn't think they would believe me. Time went on until one day, about twelve o'clock, I had left my baby sister at home and gone to the well to draw some water. As I was letting the bucket down I looked up and saw in the east part of the world the heaven open and something like an ice-pick, having four prongs, come out. A voice spoke to me. It sounded like it filled the world. It said, "You got to die and can't live again." I ran home hollering and scared and fell across a cedar chest we had. I felt myself dying. It started in my feet and came on up over my body. As it crept over me it looked like I was coming un-jointed.

When I knew anything I was standing over a gulf with my back to the east. I was leaning over looking down on X. He was fastened on some horse in hell. He turned his face from me in agony and said, "Oh, go tell the people! Don't come here!" I began to mourn and pray, and as I did a little man appeared beside me, standing in space. He spoke to me saying, "My little one, you must die for Jesus' sake." I looked, and before me was a machine with a lot of blades on it, and they were moving back and forth. He spoke again and said, "Justice cut you down, but mercy will plead your case." With this he turned my face to the east and said, "Behold yourself." I looked, and I was all dressed up. I had a golden crown on my head and sandals on my feet and a long, snow-white robe covered my body. He said, "Behold, I have dressed you up at the doors of hell, and you are ready for traveling." He then led me to the east. We came to a green pasture where there were many sheep. They were all eating until we came up. Then they all stopped at once, raised their heads, and gave one mourn.

We went on through the pasture and came to a snow-white wall with large gates. He spoke and said, "Ye everlasting gates, fly open wide for my bride!" When the gates flew apart I saw a beautiful city, the length and breadth of which I couldn't tell. There was no sun, but it was as bright as day when the sun is in midheaven. As we entered the gate I saw three roosters. They had long bills that circled under their bodies and came back over their heads. These represented preachers, and I was made to know the names of them all. One of them came out and mourned before me three times and then rushed back into the building, and I saw him no more. It was Brother B. P., and I was directed to him to be baptized. Soon after this he did baptize me and died shortly after.

As I still stood looking about me—I don't know why, but I was not afraid—a cup was handed to me, and as it touched my lips it touched the lips of a host of angels that sat at a long table of which I couldn't see the end. The voice said to me, "This is love and union."

He took me and showed me a large book and my name written in it. I also saw my seat and sat in it. It just fitted me. I tried to see the end of the city and the mansions, but I could not. As far as I could see was peace and joy and calmness.

Jesus himself baptized me, saying, "My little one, behold I have baptized you myself. I command you to go in yonder world. Open your mouth, and I will speak through you. Harken unto me, for I am able to encircle the world as an iron hand. I told you to go, and you shall go."

He showed me a vineyard with shrubs and plants of all kinds and sizes. He said, "I will bring them all in my own appointed time. Go and be of good cheer, for I will encamp round and round about you like a mighty wall, and many shall hear thee and believe. Amen."

When he finished speaking I came to myself, and it looked like I just wanted to kiss the very ground. I had never felt such a love before. Soon after this I went to Brother B. P. and told him what the Lord had done for me. He took me in and baptized me, and soon he died. I was the last person he baptized.

Since I became converted I have seen visions and many wondrous things.

Once I saw, in broad daylight, the heavens open and a man stand in midair, with one hand reaching into the heavens where sat one he called Judge. His other hand reached down to earth, and along his arm was a tape, and on it were names written, and as the tape moved a name would snap off. A voice said, "I am the Operator. Behold the Judge who sitteth on the throne of righteousness. Amen."

About two years ago, while lying in bed, I saw three suns rise in the east. A voice said, "The Father, the Son, and the Holy Ghost." I jumped out of bed, and when I came to myself I was standing before the mantel. It was about three o'clock in the morning when this happened.

a preacher from a god-fearing plantation

I was born a slave, and when the Civil War started I was about sixteen years old. Up until about three years before the war, I lived with my people on a plantation in South Carolina. My owner was a good woman, and we got along a little better than most slaves. She taught my uncle to preach, and most of the time she attended the meetings. My mother was a great shouter after she got converted, and Miss X. used to always hold her. Sometimes she would almost shout. My uncle couldn't read, so Miss X. just read off a little scripture to him, and he would stand up before us and preach away for an hour or more. I didn't know then how he could do it, but I know now. He was full of the spirit, and the words came to him from on high.

I was too small to know what these things meant to me, but as I got older and learnt a little more they all came back to me; today, as I look back over the past and recall some of the prayers I heard and remember the joy and happiness that filled the older people's hearts, I believe all the more that the seed was planted in my heart. I can never forget how my mother shouted and cried and wrung her hands for joy on the morning she was overcome by the Holy Spirit. When she fell out as if dead I was standing right over her and stayed there until she came back telling the news. Oh, she came back shouting, and as long as she lived she never stopped! It just looked like she loved everybody. She seemed to even love the very ground she walked on.

Of my own life, while I stayed with my people, there is not much to tell. As a boy I lived close to my mother, and she taught me how to live and pray and how to take care of myself. She taught me how to wash my clothes, because she was always afraid that I might be sold from her or that she might be sold and sent away from me. For this reason I was not mischievous like some boys. I don't remember but one thing that I did out of the way, and that was to rob a bird's nest one day. The old folks made me feel so bad about it that I never bothered another one.

My father was a good man, but I didn't see much of him because he belonged to different people. They let him come once a week to see us. I was always glad for him to come because he could read a little, and he taught me about all that I ever learned out of the Blueback Speller. I was anxious to learn, and I wouldn't hesitate about asking anybody to tell me something. Once in a while my mistress would let me and my cousin go over to the adjoining plantation where my father was. This gave me a chance to learn more, for the slave children over there knew more than we did. They went to a Catholic Sunday school and knew how to read a little. Whenever I went over there, there wasn't much playing for me. I got around them and asked so many questions they had to stop and tell me something. In this way I learned a little something, and by the time I was sold I had covered fifteen pages in the Blueback Speller.

I don't know why I wanted to learn so bad, unless it was because my mother prayed and cried over us so much. The old folks used to slip out in the fields and thickets to have prayer meetings, and my mother always took me along for fear something would happen to me if left behind. They would all get around a kettle on their hands and knees and sing and pray and shout and cry. My mother was a great prayer, and she always asked God to take care of her son—meaning me. I would look and listen; sometimes I would cry. I didn't know what I was crying for, but the meaning and singing was so stirring that I couldn't help it. Now, as I look back, I know that these things sunk deep in my heart.

My father started me off to praying. Every Wednesday night when he came to see us, as soon as it was time for us to go to bed, he always called me to him and made me kneel down between his knees and say my prayers. He was a powerful man, and my mother rejoiced in him so. She wouldn't do anything without first asking him. It was so joyful to see them together. He would always ask my mother if I had been a good boy. They smiled at me always and then turned away, either looking in the fire or at each other. I noticed that they always looked sad afterward, but I didn't know why. I know now though that they were thinking of what might happen to me. I know now that there was power in every look and groan. When the heart begins to bleed on the inside, and a child begins to plead with the Master, I can tell you that something is going to happen. The old slaves didn't know nothing about books, but they did know God. And knowing him they called on him in their trouble and distress, and I can testify that he heard them.

There were some things that happened when I was a boy that I will never forget. I will never forget the day I saw my mother fall out and rise again, shouting and praising God. I will never forget some of the meetings in the fields and thickets where the old folks got together in the quiet hours of the night and lifted their voices to glory. Neither can I forget the first time I heard my mistress read from the Bible and tell Uncle that Christmas was the birthday of Christ and that she wanted him to preach on the birth of our Lord. I want to tell you he preached. He set that little house on fire. Everybody was shouting and crying. My mistress took her handkerchief and wiped my mother's eyes and nose. At the close of the preaching Uncle called on Mama to pray, and she sent up a petition that moved every heart. My uncle had a good memory. After hearing the scripture read he could stand and preach for over an hour, and every word seemed to find lodgment in some heart.

At another meeting among us I remember a prayer by the white preacher that spoke that day. He got down and in a powerful, trembling voice called on God. The one thing he said that I never forget was, "Righteous God of all, remember the poor, ignorant, helpless slaves." I don't know why this stayed with me, unless it opened my eyes to my condition. I never will forget that prayer.

So this was the surroundings and kind of people I started out in life with. My family was a family of praying people, and I caught the spirit.

About three years before the war my troubles started. Up until this time I hadn't tasted any hard times, for my mistress was not so hard on her slaves. She was a Christian woman. As I think back now I wonder why she didn't free us, but I guess she thought, like all the rest, that slaves were just so much property.

I was about twelve or fourteen years old when I was sold. A Negro trader came along and bought up all the slaves he could and took us to Louisiana. About this time many people sold their slaves because they all felt the same thing was going to happen. One side thought the war would come and all the slaves get freed. All that felt this way about it began to sell, so as to get the money. There were others that thought that in case of war the South would win. They held what slaves they had and even bought more.

On the morning I was sold and went to tell my mother goodbye, she fainted. She was in the bed, and I went to the door and said, "Goodbye, Mama, goodbye." It nearly broke her heart. She just cried out, "Goodbye, son! Meet me in glory." Then she turned her face from me. I never expected to see her again in this life, but I did. It was after the war though, and I had got free and found God and was preaching the gospel.

I was taken down in Louisiana and sold. The man that bought me was the meanest man, I believe, ever God created. He whipped from about three o'clock in the morning until eight and nine o'clock at night. It was awful to hear the poor slaves crying, "Oh pray, Master." Both men and women were whipped alike. I held one old man to be whipped and saw him beat to death. I don't know how many he beat to death, but I came near being killed myself. I have a scar on my chest now as large as my fist that came from a blow he gave me with a knotted stick. He not only beat his slaves nearly to death, but he took many of the women off and cohabited with them almost in our sight. I lived through it all, praying to God every day for deliverance, and it came.

After the war I got a partner, and we started out share-cropping. I took fresh courage and began to see life a little different, but there was one thing that never left me, and that was the last promise I had made to meet my mother in glory. I had never ceased to pray, but it looked like my burden got heavier. I went around some with other boys and danced and had a good time a little, but every now and then the thought would come to me, "Remember the promise you made to your mother to meet her in glory." This thought always restrained me whenever I would attempt to go too far. I kept praying and seeking because I thought my mother was dead or, even if she wasn't dead, I didn't know that I would ever see her again. Every way I turned I found somebody looking for mother, father, sister, son, or brother. In many cases separation had been so long that brothers and sisters would meet and would not know each other. They were sold here and there and changed their names so much that it was hard for even mothers to make themselves known to their children, if lucky enough to find them.

As time went on, I heard that my mother was still alive. I worked and prayed then harder than ever, trying to save up enough money to go and look for her. I prayed and prayed, and my burden got heavier and heavier. All the time the thought kept running through my mind, "Remember the promise you made to your mother." I got so that my food didn't taste right. I could not sleep at night. I just felt heavy and burdened. My partner noticed me looking so sad and asked me what was the trouble. I told him that I was sick and that I was not going to eat anymore until I had found God. He said, "I'll be damned if you don't die." I went on this way for a day or two. I was chopping in the field. I began to feel faint and sick. It seemed that I was going to die. I called to an old lady nearby and said, "Aunt, please get some meat and meal out at our house and cook some dinner, for I believe I am going to die." (I was doing our cooking.) She said, "All right, son. Pray on, God will come after a while." These were the last words I heard. I fell to the ground and said, "Goodbye and farewell; I am going to die."

I fell sprawling out with my face to the ground. I immediately lost sight on the world. The next thing I knew I was in a helpless condition. My body lay on the brink of a great and dark pit. I heard voices crying, "Cool water! Cool water!" I realized my helplessness and surrendered. I cried out, "Lord, have mercy!"

The darkest hour of the night is just before the break of day. The darkest hours of my life as a slave came just before freedom, and in the same way, in my trials with sin, when everything seemed lost I was delivered. No sooner had I surrendered and cried out, "Lord, have mercy!" than the work was done. It seemed as if a great burden were lifted from me, and my soul took a leap and left the old body. A great light came from above, and a voice cried, "Lo, I am the way. Trust and believe." My soul took the air, and having wings like a bird I flew away into a world of light with thousands of other images like myself; all the time a voice was crying, "Peace! Peace! Peace! Free! Free! Free!"

I don't know how long the vision lasted. I don't know where my soul was, only that it was flying in a world of light, peace, and harmony. That was the greatest joy of my life. Everything was joy and peace. The voice was crying, "Peace! Peace!" and my soul was rejoicing. I don't know where the voice was coming from. I didn't see anything but myself and the other white images like me. The voice and the light filled the heavens, and as I flew I felt as light as a feather. I knew at the time that I was in another world, and I knew that I had left my earthly body behind, but whether I ever came back to it or not, I do not know. I remember looking down on my body as my soul flew away, but this is the last I remember until the heavenly vision was over; then I found myself on the ground where I first fell. I rose to my feet a new creature and went spreading the news. I have had other visions since, but this one was the one that put fire in my bones. It started me to traveling, and I haven't stopped yet. My joy through the sixty years that I preached the gospel, and up until now, is the joy that comes from remembering what a great man God is. Sometimes, now, when I sit alone in my little room and talk with him, I think of him as just a man. At other times I think of him as a great power that fills the universe.

The first thought that struck me after I had the vision in the field was that I must go and preach. I just felt like running. It was not long afterward that I preached my first sermon. They took me in the church and baptized me. On the morning I stood up to speak I did not know what I was going to say, but when I started to talk my thoughts came faster than I could speak. I was filled up. The old meeting house caught on fire. The spirit was there. Every heart was beating in unison as we turned our minds to God to tell him of our sorrows here below. God saw our need and came to us. I used to wonder what made people shout, but now I don't. There is a joy on the inside, and it wells up so strong that we can't keep still. It is fire in the bones. Any time that fire touches a man, he will jump.

I was sin-sick. I didn't eat or drink from Friday until Tuesday. I fasted Saturday, but I went to the mill with all the corn, etc. I was sick all over, and Tuesday, coming out of the field, my teeth were clenched and I was in chains of sin and I fell down by the side of a chicken coop. In twenty minutes after I had done this, the voice of God spoke to me and said, "I am the way." A light shone and darted across me, and I felt the burning of my heart, and I felt as light as a feather and began singing.

I saw myself in two parts—this body sitting over dead body. I went to the mount of Calvary and to the river of Jordan, and when I clumb Mount Calvary there were four angels around a white table, and their wings were tipped with gold, and all raised their wings at once and said, "This is heaven." Then I found myself in this world, and the trees bowed to me and said, "This is holy ground."

I saw the Lord in the east part of the world, and he looked like a white man. His hair was parted in the middle, and he looked like he had been dipped in snow, and he was talking to me. He said, "Hey, my little one, I am God Almighty, I am a wall around my people, and if I call you through fire and water, come on, follow me." He led me. I saw myself hanging over a gulf by a thread—oh, it was so dark in that pit! He brought me up out of that pit on a thread. He carried me to the east part of the world, and I saw many sheep in green pastures. Then suddenly everything got dark, and I could feel the darkness with my hands. I was just picking it up looking at it.

One night in church I was nodding, and I heard a prayer in the east part of the world, and the devil was on this side of me. I squealed and jumped and the devil talked to me, but the Lord talked deep down in my soul and said, "Go in peace and sin no more." I felt him when he cut the sin-cord loose way down in here. He gave me three pieces of ribbon.

All of my people were great Christians. Shouting, singing, praying, and good old, heartfelt religion make up the things that filled their lives. My grandmother was named Eve. She was a Christian from head to foot. It didn't take much to get her started, and when she called on God she made heaven ring.

There was Aunt Bellow, a heavy, brownskinned woman. She was a great shouter. Aunt Charlotte used to cry most all the time when she got happy. Aunt Kate was a tall, portly woman and a shouter. It took some good ones to hold her down when she got started. Any time Uncle Link or any other preacher touched along the path she had traveled she would jump and holler. It took some good ones to hold her. The old ones in them times walked over benches and boxes with their eyes fixed on heaven. God was in the midst of them.

Where there is so much smoke, there is bound to be some fire somewhere. So this is the atmosphere I came up in. It was where people feared God and called upon him with the spirit. I remember once, after the white preacher had been coming and preaching to the slaves Sunday after Sunday, Uncle Link got up in the stand. Doctor Bowman, the white preacher, taught Uncles Link and Morgan and Jacob to fill the stand when he was not able to come. (It was the custom for the plantation owners to hire a white preacher to preach to the slaves, and Doctor Bowman was our preacher.) But Uncle Link filled the stand that morning. Mistress read the scripture off to him, and he started to preaching. As he warmed up the spirit struck him and, let me tell you, they set that place on fire that day. After he finished preaching my mother prayed, and Lord! it looked like the very heaven would come down. My mother could send up the most powerful prayer of anybody on that plantation or in that part of the country. My mistress cried and took her handkerchief and wiped my mother's eyes. She said that that was the first time she had felt the presence of God since the little church had been built. I don't know how Uncle Link could preach so much, for he couldn't read the scriptures. Then the people would sing and pray. After this Uncle Link would get up on the stand, and he could remember everything she had read to him. He wouldn't talk long before the spirit would strike him, and then it was easy sailing. It looked like his very soul would catch on fire.

Meetings back there meant more than they do now. Then everybody's heart was in tune, and when they called on God they made heaven ring. It was more than just Sunday meeting and then no more godliness for a week. They would steal off to the fields and in the thickets and there, with heads together around a kettle to deaden the sound, they called on God out of heavy hearts. I was small, but I witnessed all these things. My mother always took us little ones along because she was afraid something might happen to us. Coming up in this I didn't have much more room in my life for mischief and frolicking. Life was a serious matter, and I had the seed sown in my heart while it was tender. So by the time I was sold I had about made up my mind what I was going to do. I couldn't get away from it, and even now, at times, it seems like I can hear my mother's voice ring through my soul as it did back in the dark days.

There were two kinds of marriages; one was marrying at home and the other was called marrying abroad. My mother and Aunt Jane both married abroad. By this I mean they married men who lived on a different plantation from them. To get married, all a couple had to do was go up and get the master's consent. He then sent the couple off to live together, and when the preacher made his next visit he would sanction the wedding in one way or another by offering a prayer. There was no need for license, for the owner's consent was sufficient.

In cases of matches between a man and woman on different plantations, the consent of both masters had to be gotten. If a man married abroad it meant that he wouldn't see his wife only once a week. My father used to come to see us every Wednesday night. He would stay all night and leave early in the morning.

Dr. Henderson was the doctor on our plantation, and he took care of all sickness. He was always on hand to attend the women when they gave birth to children. After giving aid and treatment, he left them in charge of some of the midwives or other women on the place. They got pretty good attention. The old heads, women too old for field work or work in the big house, usually looked after the sick. Most of the slaves around in our neighborhood lived better than they did in other places. I found this out after I was sold. I went through three years of hell while I was in Louisiana. I don't like to talk about it, but as long as I live I will never forget it, because I was sold to a devil. It was knock, kick, and a beating from sun to sun.

Just before I was sold—a year or two—I had got big enough to get about a little. I kinder got stuck on a girl once, but another fellow beat my time with her and married her. That left me out. I used to go to dances a little. I was so nimble and supple I could cut the pigeonwing as good as the best of them. It was not long before I started to prompting. I was full of life. When I hollered "swing corners" they slipped about. Dancing then was pretty when it was done right. I used to love to holler "balance all," "ladies your heads too high," "turn where your heart lies," "swing corners," "let me see the first man to the right," "honor your partner," etc. All these things the prompter had to call out, and the dancers moved like clocks. You could hear me holler a mile, and Lord! the dust would fly.

But in the midst of all this I couldn't feel free. Something had a grip on me. The seed had been planted in my heart during my early childhood, and I never could go very far without thinking back over the road and recalling some of the songs and prayers I had heard all my life. I was a gifted child, and all my life both white and black have said that I was a child of nature. Once a good brother (a preacher) told me I was a perfect conundrum. I didn't know what he meant, but as soon as I got to somebody that did know I asked him what the word meant. He told me that the brother was complimenting me and saying that I was a great mystery.

When I was small I used to dream a lot. I remember one night I dreamt that I saw Uncle Link, Uncle Jake, and Uncle Peter skinning a cow and cutting her open. A lot of women and children were sitting around and seemed to be crying. I told my mother about it the next morning. She said it was a sign of death to dream about fresh meat. Sure enough, that very evening Uncle Peter Price died. I used to dream so much that the old heads got so they took special notice of me, and nearly every time it would come true.

In case of death and funerals the slaves got off. Mr. John Hill, that owned a plantation adjoining ours, used to go out whenever there was to be a funeral among the Negroes and say to the freed slaves, "Well, old so-and-so is to be buried today at two o'clock, so you all can knock off and go to the funeral." They had funerals in them days too. The body was put on a wagon or cart and hauled to the burying ground, and the singing and shouting on the way, Lord, there was no end to it. Some were rejoicing because one of their number had been called away out of this lowland of sorrows.

On our plantation the slaves knocked off from work a little earlier on Saturdays than on other days. Saturday night was the time for everybody to clean up a little. Bathing and shaving and getting ready for Sunday were things we had to do. My mother used to put me and my brother in a washtub and wash us up and put us in clean clothes. Our master didn't allow his slaves to go without cleaning up at least once a week. Anybody that failed to do it got a whipping.

When the hands came in from the field and put the teams away, they went to the big house with their buckets to get their dram [whiskey]. Our master kept a ten- or twenty-gallon keg, and on Saturdays the slaves could go up and get a toddy.

This brings to my mind another thing about my master. He was full of fun and mischief. He used to get some of the little slave children up to the big house and make them drunk. It done him so much good to see them staggering and falling about. After he had had all the fun he wanted, he would call their mothers to come and get them and take care of them until they got sober. I don't think he meant anything wrong. He was just having fun. Considering times back then he was a good man. The old mistress was the boss, and when she was around he stepped lightly.

I remember once he was about to get on me for something, but before he hit me a lick she happened along. She told him he was not going to touch me. With that she caught him in the collar and led him to the house, and there he stayed. I made myself scarce until everything had quieted down. When he happened about the place later he was in good humor, and I never did get the whipping.

But I never did get many whippings, because I was always obedient and respected the old folks. Youngsters then had more respect than they have now. When I was a boy, if an older person spoke to me, I moved and moved quick. It was the same as if my own folks had spoken to me. If you didn't obey, they would either go on you themselves or tell your mamma and daddy, and then you had better look out.

Once I went to the spring and stayed and stayed, and my mother called and called me. When I got home she said, "Never mind, sir, I am going to make your daddy whip you when he comes home Wednesday night." I was awful tender-hearted, but like most boys I would get into a little something now and then. When my father came that Wednesday night she told him. He took me down, head between his knees, and told me to pray because he was going to whip me. I turned to Mama and said, "Mama, are you going to let Papa whip me?" They both laughed. He took me up on his knees and told me that I must be a good boy and that I must honor and obey my mother or God wouldn't love me.

I loved my father. He was such a good man. He was a good carpenter and could do anything. My mother just rejoiced in him. Whenever he sat down to talk she just sat and looked and listened. She would never cross him for anything. If they went to church together she always waited for him to interpret what the preacher had said, or what he thought was the will of God. I was small, but I noticed all these things. I sometimes think that I learned more in my early childhood about how to live than I have learned since.

I first found out that something was going to happen one day when I got back with the mail. My master took the paper I brought, and after looking at it a minute he turned to Mistress and said, "That old Yankee has got elected, and I am going to sell every nigger I got because he is going to free them."

When this news got out among the slaves there was a lot of disturbance and speculation on who would be the first one. I was a boy then big enough to work. I had a brother named John and a cousin by the name of Brutus. Both of them were sold, and about three weeks later it came my turn. Sadness filled that whole plantation. My mother just broke down and took the bed. My father came over, and they prayed and sang over me. He gave me this advice. He knew more about what was going on than we did. He had read about the war to free the Negroes. "When you get your freedom, come back and look for us. But whatever you do, treat people right; respect the old; go to meetings; and if you never more see us in this world, meet us in heaven." My father belonged to a Miss Billinger, and when she died she willed him to her nephew William. They had taught him to read and write.

My master sent me into Charleston, there to wait until fall when the prices went up. I worked there as a dragman until sold to a Negro trader. My master had a big house in Charleston where he stayed part of the year.

On the day I left home, everything was sad among the slaves. My mother and father sung and prayed over me and told me how to get along in the world. I took my little bundle of clothes—a pair of slips, a shirt, and a pair of jeans pants—and went to give mamma my last farewell. I did not see her again until after the war.

I went on into Charleston. The prices usually went up on slaves in the fall of the year. Along in September, what was known as "nigger traders" started to coming around Charleston, which was a great trading post. When selling time came we had to wash up and comb our hair so as to look as good as we could and demand a high price. Oh yes, we had to dress up and parade before the white folks until they picked the ones they wanted. I was sold along with a gang of others to a trader, and he took us to Louisiana. There, I believe, I was sold to the meanest man that God ever put breath in. Out of seventeen of us sold to him, only four of us got back home. Some died; others he killed.

At times we worked all night. We never got enough to eat. It was a shame the amount of bread and meat we had for forty or fifty of us. Sometimes we had what they called meal-soup. This was made by boiling a lot of odds and ends of meat in a lot of water, thickened with meal.

We were always in the field and at work long before sunup. Away by and by the dinner cart would come. This was a little mule and cart they used for bringing meals to us when we had to go a long way from the house to work. We stopped work just long enough to eat and maybe take a drink of water. By the time the cart got back to the house, I would be feeling like I hadn't had a bite to eat. I started to praying and calling on God, and let what come that might. I somehow found time and a chance to slip to the bushes and ask God to have mercy on me and save my soul.

My master hated Lincoln because he thought he was going to help the slaves. When we were set free, he didn't tell us a thing about it. When Congress sent out the order for all the slaves to be set free, we didn't know a thing about it until a man came and told us. Our master was scared that we would run away, so he tried to keep strict watch on us.

Most of us did finally run away, a few at a time. I remember the night me and some more slipped away. We had to go through a pea patch. The vines were all over it, and we had an awful time getting through there! We went on to Colonel Wilson's house because this was a kind of headquarters for freed slaves. We slept on the porch until next morning. Colonel Wilson hired us all to work for him at five dollars a month. Lord, we would have been glad to work for him for nothing, we felt so glad to be free.

Seventeen of us ran away to freedom the first night, and the next night twenty-three ran off and came where we were and, Lord, if we didn't shout when we heard that everybody was leaving. The next day old man MacMillan and his son Billy came riding up to the colonel's house. Some of the hands got scared, but the colonel said, "Keep still. They can't do nothing to you. By the Lord Almighty, you are as free as I am." Old man MacMillan and Billy came on up. Colonel Wilson invited them to sit down and sent out and got them something to drink. After a while the colonel said to them, "Well, gentlemen, what is your business here this morning?" They said, "We are out looking for some of the hands. A lot of them ran away, and we didn't know it until this morning, when we checked up and found some of them missing." Colonel Wilson turned to Jack Gorman, the man who was working with him. Gorman was sitting in the door with his head in his hands, like he wasn't noticing anything at all. When the colonel spoke to him he raised his head and turned around and said, "Well, gentlemen, the Congress of the United States told me to look out for all the Negroes that came to me for protection, and by God I am going to do it." Well, sir, you ought to have heard us Negroes shouting when we saw old man MacMillan and his son going away like whipped dogs.

We stayed on with Colonel Wilson until the harvest was over. Then Jack Gorman rented a cotton field, and we harvested that. Later Gorman and Bill (Colonel Wilson's son-in-law) bought old Scroggins' farm. Scroggins had to sell because he didn't have enough hands to save his crop. This was in the years 1865–67. In 1867 we went to the Bell farm and worked for him two years. He paid us by the year. After these two years I went to Texas.

Up until the time I was sold down in Louisiana I didn't know what hard times were, but from the first day I got on that plantation my troubles began, and they lasted until I got free. I was a young boy and had never done much work. About the time I was sold I had just started to driving a cart about the place—hauling wood and trash and doing odd jobs. Aside from this, I used to take care of the slave babies while the parents were in the field at work. So I hadn't done any work like I had to do in Louisiana.

Ever since I got freed I have been trying to figure what made that man so mean. As I look back over it now, I don't wonder that I felt as I did. I just gave up all earthly hopes and thought all the time about the next life. Though I suffered then from hardships, and though I still have pains from this scar, I hold no hatred towards anybody. I have always said that that man was a devil on earth, but I have forgiven him. The same God that made the good made the evil, and I guess he knows what is best. After thinking about this man, I have come to believe that he was so mean because he felt that the war was coming and that we would be freed. You see, some foresaw the war and the freedom of the slaves, while others didn't. He was one who thought that in case of war the South would win. So he bought slaves while everybody else was selling theirs. When he saw that war was coming, he got harder and harder. He was as hard on the women as the men. Some of the things I saw him do to women is too low to tell. At times I look back over the road I have traveled and wonder how I am still here.

I came out of a praying family, and I believe that God heard my people when they called on him. All my uncles and aunts were prayers. I don't remember my grandfather. His master gave him to his son. They went off to live, and I never saw him again. I remember some of my uncles and aunts. My father's name was Harry Green. He belonged to an old maid; her name was not Green, but he just took that name. He used to sing a song all the time when he came to see Mama. The song was "Jesus, my all, to heaven has gone." He would sing that, and my mother would almost shout. I used to watch them when they sat and talked.

One day, while I was over to see my father, I went in with the rest of the children to read the catechism. When my father's mistress found out that I couldn't read, she called my father and told him that he would have to buy me a book. He promised to do it and did. One of the last things he said to me was, "Son, here is a Blueback Speller. Keep it with you as long as it lasts, and when it wears out buy another one." I kept it for years and years.

I never went to school a day in my life, but once while I was in Texas—this was after the war—I taught some children how to read and spell. There wasn't no schools and teachers, but many of the old people that had got freed and had children wanted them to learn something. So anybody that could read and write a little would take a few children and teach them. Nobody was able to pay much. About a dollar a month was all you would get.

I don't know how I came to preach my first sermon, but I felt that I had been ordained of God to preach the gospel even though I couldn't read and write.

On the Sunday following the day that me and God met, I went to the little church (an old blacksmith shop that the white folks allowed us to worship in) and was received into the flock, baptized after telling what God had done for me, and invited to preach on the following Sunday. I went back rejoicing. I got up before the congregation not knowing what I was going to say. I stepped to the front and just hung my head and cried. I was so full and overjoyed that I couldn't help but cry. After it was over I told the brethren to excuse me, but I was just so happy that I couldn't keep back the tears. I started to preaching. I don't remember much what I said, but I do know that I set that place on fire. The shouting and jumping went on the whole time I stood there.

This was my trial sermon. I was ordained a minister of the gospel soon afterward, and because of the way the brethren shouted and rejoiced over my first sermon I gained faith and confidence. For twelve years after I was ordained I worked and preached about in the different churches and meeting houses, until I was appointed to take care of a large number of the little flocks scattered over the country. There wasn't many preachers, so one man often had to pastor a large number of the little flocks.

These years that I speak of now were spent in Texas, and it is said of me that I carried Texas as a storm. Whenever it was announced that Green was going to preach they came flocking from all directions, both white and colored. I was full of fire and never failed to touch somebody's heart.

I wore out my spelling book and bought another one. About this time I was beginning to feel myself much of a man. I was preaching the gospel and praising God every day. One day a white man that had heard me preach came to me, and after we had talked a long time he noticed my thirst for knowledge. He commented on how much more I knew than most of the preachers he had heard. I told him how I had come to know what I did. When he was ready to leave he took a piece of paper and wrote this sentence: "George Washington was the first president of the United States." He then read it to me and told me to copy it over and over, until I could write it as good as he had written it. I copied it and studied on it until I could do fairly well. My biggest trouble came in trying to join the letters together. After I caught onto the knack of it I went sailing. It was hard to find anybody that could do much reading and writing back in them days.

The old folks couldn't read and write, but they wanted their children to get some little education. I didn't teach long because of my ministerial duties. I started to traveling then, and I swept the country as I went. All over the South, West, and as far north as Kansas, the name of Green got to be a byword. Whenever I stood up before a congregation there was some preaching done. I was so full of fire. I just went running without parse of script, and I was filled with the Holy Ghost.

During the whole number of years I was preaching, I never took any thought of money or how I would fare in life. I have never had anything, but I have never been in want. God knows the needs of them that trust him. Even now I feel his care. He has opened up the heart of somebody to take me in now. It is through his mercies that I am living today in comparative ease and comfort. I made no preparation for this day, but he, being all-wise, looked ahead and foresaw the very day when people that I had never seen nor heard of would take me up, an old, helpless man, and put me in a place of honor. I give all the thanks to God, because I can feel his power and goodness in everything.

My master's house was a big, nine-room, frame house located in Colinton district about forty miles west of Charleston. A big road separated this plantation from the neighboring one. The house was built on brick rocks and sills as a foundation. It was only one story high, but it had all these rooms and a kitchen with three rooms to it. The kitchen was connected to the big house by a shed. The kitchen had a big, long, home-made table in the center. At one end of the room was a big fireplace. There was no stove. To cook bread, the cook put it in a skillet and pulled out a lot of hot embers under it. Then she covered it over and put hot coals on top. We had a long rod to lift the lid, to keep the food from burning. This was my job sometimes. I was what you call the waiting-boy, doing all kinds of little odd jobs about the house—sweeping, dusting, waiting on table, opening the gate for the carriage, and, in general, doing a little bit of everything. I used to shine my master's shoes and ride behind him, at times, when he was hunting. I carried his gun and got all such game as he might kill.

My master was one of those "high-toned" people. He kept a plenty of good whiskey and always had a plenty of company. They danced, played cards, drank, and did everything. Whenever there was a big party we had to jump about. Sometimes the old cook would have to cook a second supper at eleven or twelve o'clock at night. And another such eating, drinking, laughing, and dancing you never heard. If the work got too heavy for us servants that stayed around the house all the time, we would call in some of the other women and field hands to help.

After the feasting was about over, the slaves would be called up to dance and sing. A white man by the name of Sneed used to furnish the music. He taught Uncle Scipio. (He was not my real uncle, but all of the older people were uncle and aunty to us youngsters.) This man taught my uncle Scipio to play the fiddle and Uncle Joshua the banjo, and they played too. I never will forget one song they always played, and that was "The Arkansas Traveler." This was the white folks' favorite, and whenever they struck up that tune, let me tell you, there was some dancing done. Usually we slaves sat around on the fence and boxes and stumps and watched them dance.

The houses that the slaves lived in were all built in a row, away from the big house. Just at the head of the street, and between the cabins and the big house, stood the overseer's house. There was some forty or fifty of these two-room cabins facing each other across an open space for a street. In them we lived. There was not much furniture. Just beds and a table, and some stools or boxes to sit on. Each house had a big, open fireplace for heat and cooking.

Some of the houses were built out of planks, and others out of logs and chinked with mud. Most of the slaves were married, so each room had its family. The beds were made to the walls. This was done by nailing a strip along the wall and then nailing a head and footpiece to it. The next thing to do was to stand two pieces of plank a few feet out from the wall, and fasten these two pieces to it and then a frontpiece. Across the center would be a lot of board strips to hold up the tick.

During the day there wasn't anybody around the quarters as a general thing. Everybody was at work in the field, the big house, or in the sewing house. This sewing house stood off from the rest. It was in here that the women did the weaving and spinning and making clothes. We got two issues of clothes every year, one in summer and one in winter. This was for women and men, and included shoes and all. I think the shoes were bought in Charleston. They used to make little black caps for us children. This they did by taking some cloth and shaping it to fit our heads and sewing on a little leather bib.

Some of us children that were too small to go to the field had to stay around and take care of the slave babies. This was my job at times. Whenever the babies got to crying too much, I would go and call their mothers from the field to come and suckle them.

At night, especially in the summertime, after everybody had eaten supper, it was a common thing for us to sit outside. The old folks would get together and talk until bedtime. Sometimes somebody would start humming an old hymn, and then the next-door neighbor would pick it up. In this way it would finally get around to every house, and then the music started. Soon everybody would be gathered together, and such singing! It wouldn't be long before some of the slaves got happy and started to shouting. Many of them got converted at just such meetings. There was so much fire among them when they started to praying and shouting, clapping and shaking hands and shedding briny tears, something had to move. One favorite song they used to sing was: "Oh, Brother, I love Jesus for his name's so sweet./I'm just now from the fountain. His name's so sweet." Another one was: "Oh the keys, oh the keys, Lord." Then somebody would holler, "Steady yourselves, children. My God! The keys! Let's find them tonight." As soon as the white folks heard the singing and shouting they came running. They would sit and listen until everything got quiet. Sometime they would ask Uncle Link or the others to sing a favorite song they liked to hear. Then everybody went to bed.

Our plantation was considered to be the most religious of any in that part of the country. It was the custom for the slaves to take turns about in going from one plantation to the other on different Sundays to hold meetings, and always, when it was the day to come to our farm, they came in flocks. And the shouting and singing, Lord! They would set that place on fire. Some of the slave-owners adjoining us let their slaves go a little more freely than others. The Haywoods, Zellers, and Hendersons were big slave-owners, and they let their Negroes mingle pretty freely. They had so much liberty we called them free Negroes.

I think the whole ring of us lived better than most slaves in other places. My master never did whip much. I have seen him call up somebody for a strapping, and then he wouldn't give it to him. You see it was the custom for a slave that was to be whipped to fall on his knees and pray, saying, "Oh pray, Master." He would say, "Get up and go to the devil." The only time I ever saw him whip anybody was when he whipped Uncle Alex for letting the mare run away and tear up a buggy.

He wouldn't have whipped him, I don't believe, if Uncle Alex had got on his knees. He caught Uncle Alex in a lie. Uncle Alex said that he was taking the mare out and had unfastened the traces on one side and had started around to the other side to unloose that one. The mare got scared when he started around her. She had on a blind bridle. (This is a bridle that has two flaps on each side to keep a horse from looking back, I reckon.) But this wasn't what made her run away. What did it was that he went and pushed up the top of the buggy before taking her out, and the sudden noise scared the mare and made her run away. I knew that Uncle Alex told a lie, because when we caught the mare she had torn the buggy all to pieces, but she was dragging the shaves and both of the traces were still fastened. I don't know why Uncle Alex told that lie and stuck to it. My master cried and almost begged him to get on his knees and say, "Pray, Master," and tell him the truth, but he wouldn't do it. He whipped him twice.

My master was a funny man. He liked to drink and have a good time. He hardly ever bothered any of us unless he was drinking. But Lord, when he started to drinking he was worrisome. He would pass down through the quarters or the barn with his whip (buggy whip) in his hand, and if he got close to you he would almost raise you sky-high. We would always run and try to keep out of his way. Whenever he started to drinking that way Mistress would catch him and take him to the house. We wouldn't see him no more for days. Then he would be all right. It was a long time before I found out what she did to keep him quiet, but as I got big enough to paddle around the house I learned the secret. She would catch him in the collar and lead him to his bed. Then she would pour the liquor to him. She would just soak him until he was too drunk to move. He wasn't no more bother then for days. She was the boss on that place. She bossed him, and he obeyed her just like a child. When he got sober he would be all right for maybe a month or more until he wanted to start drinking again. Every time, she would give him the same treatment.

So in my early life I didn't know so much about hard slave life. We lived better than most slaves. We had preaching and singing. All of my family were God-fearing, and I came up in an atmosphere charged with faith, hope, and the Holy Spirit. Outwardly we sung; inwardly we prayed.

I didn't mean to get off here, but God has been so good to me I can't help it. I just must praise his name. I think of an old song that we used to sing, and the Negroes would almost lift the top off of the house. "I am just now from the fountain. His name's so sweet."

What I was going to say, before I got off, was one other thing about my master. He was a good man, but he was pretty bad among the women. Married or not married made no difference to him. Whoever he wanted among the slaves, he went and got her or had her meet him somewhere out in the bushes. I have known him to go to the shack and make the woman's husband sit outside while he went in to his wife. Of course, marriage among the slaves was different from what it is now. Then, it wasn't much more than the master giving consent. They usually did this readily, because they wanted the slaves to couple off. So I don't know how big a sin it was for my master to go among the women freely. I used to ride behind him on horseback, and whenever he went to see a woman he would leave me with the horse along beside the big road, and he would go a little distance into the bushes and thickets —far enough from the big road to be out of sight. If whoever he had told to be there was not there, he would wait around until she came. He would come back after so long a time, get on his horse, and go on his way either back home or wherever he started to go. I am not accusing him of nothing, but these are just things that I saw. He wasn't no worse than none of the rest. They all used their women like they wanted to, and there wasn't nobody to say anything about it. Neither the men nor the women could help themselves. They submitted to it but kept praying to God.

i want you to jump

When the Lord first started to work with me I couldn't eat and I couldn't sleep. I just wanted to be alone. I just felt burdened down. I tried to sing it off or talk it off, but got no relief. I said, "Lord, what do you want me to do?" He said, "Just one little thing I want you to do: I want you to jump."

One night I saw an angel dressed in a long white robe flying in the east with a little infant behind. She said to me, "Come on!" I told my daddy about it, and he said it was God.

When I was killed dead I saw the devil and the fires of hell. The flames were blue and green. I left hell and came out pursued by the devil. God came to me as a little man. He came in my room and said, "Come on and go with me." He was dressed in dark, but later he came dressed in white and said, "Come, and I will show you paradise and the various kinds of mansions there." I saw the most beautiful rooms, all in white and gold. There was a stream flowing through every room. He said, "This is the living water that flows from on high." He told me to taste it. It was the best-tasting water I ever drank. I can't say what kind of water it was, but I never tasted anything like it. It was as clear as it could be.

He carried me through all the rooms and said, "Go in peace and sin no more. Keep fighting and look the way the Lamb has gone." I said, "Thank the Lord! Thank the Lord!"

The devil, his face as black as it could be and his eyes as red as fire, told me to come and go with him, and that if I followed God I would lose all my friends. But I said to the devil to leave me alone, and that I had promised to follow Jesus.

I didn't know which church I wanted to join. I kinder wanted to go to the Methodist because I was afraid to be baptized. I said, "Lord, take this fear from me." And he spoke to me and said, "Trust me for one thing, trust me for all. I will take away all your fear."

At times my burden seems heavy, but he told me one day, "My little one, I will not put any more on you than you can stand. I work when no man can hinder. I have overcome the world." Ever since then, when the Lord freed my soul, I have been rejoicing.

When the spirit strikes me I lose all sense of the world. Once I had a sore foot, and I could hardly stand to put it to the floor. I lived very near the church, and one night they had a prayer meeting there. I managed to creep out on my porch to hear. I listened for a long time and tried to keep still, but it just looked like the more I tried to be still the funnier I felt. I kept getting happier and happier until I forgot all about the sore foot and ran over to the church. I scared them all, for they thought I was unable to walk. I entered the church talking and testifying of God. As soon as I got through I was satisfied. I came out, and it was not until the next day that I thought of my foot and how sore it was. The spirit makes us move about and forget all our troubles.

to hell
with a
prayer in
my mouth

The Lord blessed me with fourteen children, and not one of them ever gave me any trouble. I brought them up to fear God. Whenever they went out at night, even after they got old enough to take care of themselves, I would never go to bed until they came in or I knew where they were. I married when I was thirteen years old, and I lived with my husband twenty-nine years.

The Lord first spoke to me when I was twelve years old. I used to see my mother pray, and I wondered what it meant. I began to pray. A voice spoke to me one day, and God called me by my name saying, "You got to die and can't live!" I married at the age of thirteen and began to be a mother. I prayed more than ever. I began to pray for my soul more and more and began to hurry God. He gave me the gift in his own time. He was drawing me all the time, but I didn't know it.

When he started to working with me right I couldn't stay in my house. It just looked like every way I turned I could hear the voice. My husband rented one house after another, but I would no sooner enter than the Lord would begin to work with me, saying each time, "You got to die and can't live!" I hadn't yet learnt anything about a spiritual death, so I thought he meant I would have to die a natural death.

My husband and neighbors thought I had lost my mind, so they sent for my mother. She came and told me to pray. At that very minute I was praying on the inside, "Lord, have mercy on me. Lord, have mercy on me." After she came I picked out a place a little way from the house, in a thicket, and then I went daily to pray. But it seemed like the more I prayed, the worse I got. I felt like I had the burden of the world on my shoulders.

Finally one night I went out to a spot much farther away from the house and fell on my knees. A voice spoke and said, "Lo, here is the way." I heard a noise like a rising storm, but I stayed there, and when the voice spoke I stretched out flat on the ground. God spoke to me and again said, "My little one, you got to die and can't live." I jumped up and went to the house and found my husband and children asleep. I got in bed, my heart still praying, "Lord, have mercy on my soul." The voice spoke again, "You got to die and can't live." I began to die right there and was dying all night. My husband called in five doctors to me, and they gave me up and said that I would not live until twelve o'clock the next day.

About nine or ten the next day I began to see the wondrous works of God. I saw myself on the very brink of hell. I was on a little something that was swinging back and forth, and it looked as if I must surely fall at any minute. My jaws were locked and my tongue clove to the roof of my mouth, but on the inside I was still praying, 'Lord, have mercy! Lord, have mercy on my soul! If it be your will to send me to hell, send me with a prayer in my mouth."

When I said this I took hope, for the Lord spoke to me and said, "I am the way, the truth, and the life. I am the very door to the Father. Follow me! Follow me!"

We journeyed on, and I came to a city the likes of which I had never beheld. There were mansions there, and in the walls I saw, as if linked and joined together, the children of God. While I was viewing the city a voice came to me saying, "Go into yonder world and tell them what a dear savior you have found." I didn't want to leave. I said, "Lord, they won't believe me if I go." He said, "I command you to go, and you shall go. Speak, and I will speak through you." Ever since that day I have been falling down and getting up, always looking to God because he promised to never leave me alone or forsake me. I am always forewarned of trouble. When he speaks to me now in the spirit, I move and move with certainty.

I lost a dear son not long ago, but before he left he told me to meet him in midair. One day not long after he died I was sitting in the room, and he appeared before me and said, "Mama, don't you know me?" I said, "No." He said, "Mama, don't you know your own son?" When he said this my soul caught on fire. I reached to grab him to my bosom again and again, but each time he got out of my reach. I said, "Oh, my son, you will drown in there. Come to Mama!" He said, "Oh no, Mother. I will not drown. I am just bathing my soul."

I have never been sick in my life but once, and then I got so frail I prayed to the Lord to take me home. He spoke to me saying, "All sickness is not unto death. When I command you to stand, stand and stand fast, for I have the reins in my own hand." I saw myself sailing along in midair one day, and when I leave this world I am going to take the wings of the morning and go into the building where there is eternal joy. Amen and thank God.

souls piled up like timber

It gives me pleasure to talk about God, for he has done so many wonderful things. I could not, if I would, refrain from talking about him. How he has dealt with others I do not know, but I do know what he has done for me.

My parents taught me to fear God from my early childhood. Once while at Fisk University I got sick, and while I was lying in a bed a little child came to my bedside and got his hand in mine and said, "Fear not, for lo! I am with you always." Then like a flash he vanished. But those words rang through my soul.

In due time I got married, after I had left school, but I continued to pray, asking God to use me according to his will. He began to talk and reveal himself to me. One night, while I was cooking supper, I suddenly got very lonely and felt burdened down. I stopped cooking, got my Bible, and sat down to read. Shortly after I started I lost sight of the world and saw myself (in the spirit) being led down a dark and lonely road, and as I went down the road it seemed to close behind me. I was praying inwardly to God saying, "Lord, have mercy!" For some reason I was caused to look up, and I saw a light on my right. I said, "Lord, where am I?" He answered, "The road you are on leads to hell, but the road on your right leads to heaven."

I looked down that dark pathway and saw what he called "the gulf of despair." I looked again and saw, as it were, human souls piled like timber, and everything was gloom and sadness.

I cried to the Lord to deliver my soul, and he lifted me from that gulf of darkness and started me to traveling on the upward road.

Again a voice spoke to me saying, "Go tell your husband that the wages of sin is death but the gift of God is eternal life. Go, and as you go, take your Bible and cry aloud." I cried unto him, and he said, "I am with you always and have taken care of you from your earliest existence." When he told me to speak to my husband I was so moved that I got up in the night and awakened him and told him what the Lord had said.

I can never tell all that I have seen and heard, for he has been so good to me. Once I prayed and said, "Lord, you have been so good to me." A voice answered, "Yes, I have been good to you. I stayed the hand of your enemies like as I stayed the hand of Abraham when he would have slain his son Isaac."

At another time my little girl was very sick, and I prayed that I might die rather than to see her suffer or lose her. It was in the morning and the sun was shining bright when a voice said to me, "Lo, thine eyes shall behold Jerusalem, a quiet habitation. Get your business fixed, for your daughter goes Sunday morning." Sure enough, she left me.

The Lord pacified my mind, and I was ready to give her up. She came back to me one day and stood right before the fire and said, "Mama, when I died you were glad." I said, "Yes," and then I said, "No." I was uncertain just how to answer, but she looked at me and said, "Mama, I like it, for it is nice here." She disappeared out of sight then.

On another occasion, when I was about to become a mother, my mother appeared before me. She frightened me, and I jumped. To her question I answered both "Yes" and "No." I told her that I didn't know her at first. She said, "Don't forget the old folks." Then she vanished.

I can never tell all I know, that I am an instrument in God's hand and with him I am not afraid to get up and go in the darkest hours of midnight. I have been a trained nurse for years, and often I have gone to work and pray for patients and seen them through after the doctors have given them up for dead. I always take Doctor Jesus with me and put him in front, and if there is any hope he lets me know.

He is a God past finding out. He hears our every cry and interprets our every groan. He never leaves one of his children ignorant.

behold
the travail
of your
soul

I am sixty-five years old and in very good health. I was born into a large family in Davidson County and was never in slavery. My parents were good Christians, and they took me to church every Sunday. I heard a great deal of shouting and preaching, but I thought mostly of amusements like dancing. I had to work hard every day in the field and at home, but I was always taught to thank God for his blessings—life and the daily food. I began to long for the peace of rest called heaven, but I was told that God had a chosen people and called whomsoever he chose. I began to pray, but I still continued to serve the devil, of whom I was very much afraid. Finally I decided that I was no good and gave up praying entirely.

One day, a year later, I was out chopping in the field. The corn was high and the weather was hot. I was feeling joyous and glad for I wanted to eat, and I was thinking of the coming dance and the good time I was going to have. Suddenly I heard a voice. It called, "Mary! Mary!" It sounded so sweet, and it seemed to ring all through me. I looked all around the field, but I saw not a single person and was alone. I suddenly became weak and faint and fell to the ground unconscious. While I lay in this condition, the voice spoke to me again and said, "My little one, I am God Almighty. I have loved you from the foundation of the world, even with an everlasting love. I have freed your soul from hell, and you are free indeed. You are the light of the world. Go and tell the world what great things God has done for you and lo, I am with you always. Behold the travail of your soul."

I looked, and lo and behold, there were two Marys! There is a being in a being, a man in a man. Little Mary was standing looking down on old Mary, on this temple, my body, and it lay on the very brink of hell. There was a deep chasm filled with ravenous beasts, and old Satan was there with a ball and chain on his leg. He had a great ball in his hand and threw this at me, but it missed me and fell far on the other side of the narrow path. I became afraid and became faint again, and there began a crying on the inside, saying, "Mercy! Mercy! Mercy, Lord!" Then I began to cry, and as I wept I looked, and there by my side stood a little man, very small and with waxen hair. His eyes were like fire, his feet as burnished brass. On his shoulder he carried a spear, and on the end of it was a star that outshone the morning sun. I saw the real sun go down, and there was great darkness, and I began to tremble with fear, but the little man spoke and said, "Be not afraid, but follow me, for lo, I am a swift messenger and will ever be thy guide. Keep thy feet in the straight and narrow path and follow me, and all the demons in hell shall not be able to cause thee to stumble or to fall."

I journeyed on and finally came face to face with God. He was seated on a high throne, and a multitude of angels hovered round and about him. As I came up my guide vanished, and I saw God. He looked neither to the right nor to the left. As I entered all the angels heaved, and in one cry they moaned, "Welcome! Welcome! Welcome! Welcome to the house of God!" I looked to the right and left and beyond the throne, and behold! I saw a beautiful green pasture, and grazing there were thousands of sheep, and they turned towards me and all in one bleat cried out, "Welcome! Welcome to the house of God." I fell at the throne of God, and a voice began to cry on the inside, "Unworthy! Unworthy!" I began to weep, and lo! an angel came out, and with a bloodstained garment wiped my tears away and said unto me, "Weep not, for behold! thou hast found favor with God." I stood up on my feet, and there was a great silence. Then one of the angels nearby said, "Behold the Lamb of God, even he who was slain from the foundation of the world." I looked, and there, coming up from the east, I saw Jesus coming with great power, having on his breastplate, buckler, and shield; and his face outshone the sun. He spoke, and out of his mouth came fire. A great smoke enveloped him, and he cried with a loud voice, "Behold! I have overcome both hell and death and the grave and henceforth I am at the right hand of power. Peace on earth and goodwill, for I have removed the sting of death and robbed the grave of her victory."

I do not remember how long I was in this state, for immediately I regained consciousness I began to shout and cry. I rushed to the house, my body all drenched in perspiration and my clothes torn from my body. I shouted the rest of the day and thought no more of the coming dance. I went to church on the following Sunday, having been directed in the spirit to an old preacher named Reverend Mason who, after hearing my testimony, reached me among his flock.

At times, though, I became slack, being tempted by old Satan. Whenever the spirit moved me to do something I felt very heavy, and if I did not go as I felt I ought to go, a great fear would come over me and a voice that seemed loud enough for everyone to hear would cry on the inside, "Remember, I have called you with a holy call, and for your disobedience I will chastise you, and you shall go."

Up to the very present time I am guided by the voice from within. I claim that unless one has heard God's voice—felt his love—in other words, unless one has had his soul freed from hell in such a way that he knows it, one would remain a sinner, and in heaven there is no room for a sinner.

Once I saw a huge image in the form of a man carved out of marble. His head lay in the east; his length and breadth were too great to comprehend. Out of his stomach came a little man who spoke in a soft voice saying, "Behold, I lay in Zion a stone, a tried stone. I am a rock in a weary land, and a shelter in the time of storm. He that prays to me shall never perish. Amen."

times
got worse
after
the war

I was born in Williamson County. When the war started, I was about fifteen years old. I got my age from my old mistress. My master gave me to my mistress when I was a little boy. I remember when he carried me to her and said, "Here is a little nigger. If you can raise him, you can have him." I was sick with the fever. She put me to bed in the big house, and she used to come in to see about me all through the night. After the war started, I ran off and joined the army. During the war I saw my mistress. She came to me and said, "Don't you remember how I nursed you when you were sick, and now you are fighting against me." I said, "No, ma'am, I am not fighting against you. I am fighting for my freedom."

I was raised without either mother or father, but at the age of twenty-one years I had bought and paid for a home, all but seven dollars. I often tell my boys that they don't know what life is. I have been through more than either of them can ever hope to go through. I was wounded in the war, but I didn't let this stop me. I kept going.

There used to be some awful times during slavery days. Work! Work! Work! from dawn to dusk. But in spite of all the work and strictness, some of the slaves used to slip from place to place after night and find a little pleasure. But woe be unto you if the paddyrollers caught you out after dark without a pass.

One night, all the older slaves on our plantation slipped off to a dance. I was young, too young to go, but I went along anyway. While everybody was having a time dancing, I espied somebody slipping up from the thicket beyond. I was sitting by the fire, but I was afraid to say anything. Soon a whole band of paddyrollers were on horses, and they almost overtook some of us. We snatched some grapevines from the trees and stretched them across the road. When they rode into these they did such cursing and swearing as you never heard. We all got home and into bed in no time.

The next morning some of them came around inquiring about who of us had been out the night before. They met me as I was on my way to the mill and recognized me. When they started questioning me, I told them I wasn't there and didn't know nothing about it. One of them caught me from the mule and told me if I didn't tell they would tie me and give me forty lashes. I was stubborn, but when they commenced tying me I started to belching. I told on everybody. I know it was wrong, but I did it to save my own hide. Nobody got any whipping, but that was the last time I got to go along with them to a frolic.

There was one old man on the plantation that everybody feared. He was a good worker, but he didn't allow anybody to whip him. Once he was up for a whipping, and this is the way he got it. Our young master got a whole gang of paddyrollers and hid them in a thicket. Then he told old man Jack that he had to be whipped. "I won't hit you but a few licks," he told him. "Papa is going away, and he sent me to give you that whipping he told you about." Old man Jack said, "Now, I won't take nairy a lick." Young Master took out a bottle of whiskey, took a drink, and gave the bottle to old man Jack and told him to drink as much as he wanted. Old man Jack loved whiskey, and he drank it all. Soon he was so drunk he couldn't hardly stand up. Young Mars' called to the men in hiding, "Come on down; I got the wild boar." They whipped the old man almost to death. This was the first and last time he ever got whipped.

He was mean, but he was a slick one. He got mad one day with one of the red steers he was plowing, and he took a rock and knocked him cold. He dragged him a little way off and told me to run to the house and tell the boss that one of his steers was awful sick. They never did know why that steer died. My mistress tried in every way to make me tell her what happened to cause the steer to die, but the old man had warned me not to tell.

We used to be always killing a shoat or something. We had to do it, for they didn't give us much to eat. A lot of gravy from fried meat, but not much meat. One day old Jack and some others killed a shoat. The boss found it out and came around to raise the devil, but old man Jack spoke up and said, "I killed that shoat and ate him up. I work hard for you every day, and you don't provide enough to eat for us. That is why I killed him."

He was funny too, and if he ever made up his mind not to do a thing, all hell couldn't change him. He would get out of it in one way or another. Once the mistress wanted him to drive her to church on Sunday morning. When the message came to him he swore he wouldn't drive, and she sent for him. We all laughed at him because we thought he surely would have to go. But while he was talking to her he let his knife slip and cut his hand right between the first finger and the thumb. "There now, I have ruined my hand standing here whittling." Mistress excused him from driving. He went back to his house, and such laughing I never heard as he told us how he outwitted her.

The only good times I had was on Sundays. Of course I wouldn't call them good times now, for it wasn't nothing but a part-day rest from work. You see, a man's measure of a thing depends on what he can get. Where it is work, work all the time, a few hours rest may mean as much as two or three days if you know how to use it. It is just like a drowning man grabbing a straw. A little time to set around and talk on Sunday seemed like a picnic to us. I often tell my boys they don't know what a hard time is like. I have gone for days without a morsel to eat, and still worked hard and felt myself much of a man.

I remember the first quarter I ever made. I got hold of a peck of sweet potatoes and took them to an old white man on the Liberty Pike. He gave me twenty-five cents for them.

I felt rich. The next time I took him a sack of roasting ears, and he gave me another quarter. I just knew I was rich then. I just kept my hand in my pocket, feeling it.

I ran off from my master when I was about fifteen years old and joined the army. I was in the field shucking corn on the Murfreesboro Pike. All at once I heard a band playing. Everybody in the field broke and ran. Not a man was left on the place. We all went and joined the army. The captain asked what we wanted, and who our master was. We told him who our master was, and that we had come to join the army. He sent us back to work on a fort they were building. When we finished this, I was sent along with others to work on Fort Negley in Nashville. I didn't work there no more than about three weeks before they started to recruiting colored soldiers. I was sent to Tullahoma for training. This was the biggest thing that ever happened in my life. I felt like a man, with a uniform on and a gun in my hand. Some of the old men couldn't learn how to do nothing. The officer of the day used to come around to inspect our uniforms and our arms. When he came along each man was to come to "present arms" and hand his piece to him. When he was through he would throw the gun back at you. One day he was inspecting old man Ike, an old man and very nervous. When the officer of the day came to him he snatched his gun to "present arms," and instead of handing it to the officer of the day he threw it at him. The gun hit him right square in the face and almost knocked him down. "There, by God, you have almost killed me," the officer said. "Sergeant, take this man out of ranks and teach him how to handle his arms."

I used to have to do guard duty a lot. They had instructed me to challenge everybody that came along. One night Lieutenant J. was on duty, and he tried to test me out. You see, they had court-martialed a man for letting the officer of the day come in on him and take his gun away from him. So this kept me on my guard when Lieutenant J. came up. That night I halted him and asked for the countersign. He gave the signal but kept coming. I recognized his voice, but I thought I would teach him a lesson. When he got nearly to me, I hollered out, "I told you to halt, goddamn you, and if you advance another step I will bore a hole clear through you." With this I pulled back the hammer, "click," on my rifle. You ought to have heard him hollering, "It's me, Sergeant, it's me." I made him get down on his hands and knees and crawl every step of the way to me. The next day the colonel sent for me. I thought I was going to catch hell, but instead he praised me for what I had done.

Lieutenant J. got even with me though. One day Squire X. told me to come to his house and get some fruit. But while I was on my way to his house, I met Lieutenant J. riding with some ladies. "Where are you going?" he asked me. "I am on the way to Squire X.'s house," I told him. "Well, you just turn right around and double-time it back to the guardhouse." I hit up a trot before him. He made the sergeant put me under arrest. It was a serious offense to leave camp without a pass, but I wanted to get off as light as possible, so I made up my mind to make like I didn't know any better. We had a good captain. He was from Missouri, and for some reason he took a special liking to me. When they took me up and tried me I said, "Captain, just give me a chance to say one word. Squire X. told me to come to his house and he would give me some fruit, because one day I gave him some coffee. I was hungry, and I thought it wouldn't mean any harm if I went and got a little snack to eat and some fruit. This is my first wrong. Can't you be a little light on me?" All he did was to put me on a detail to dig up some stumps for a few days. The lieutenant and others got it in for me because I got off so easy, and whenever there was any detail guard duty or hard work they put it on me. The old, married men didn't like me because I had such a good hand with the captain.

Whenever I wanted anything I always went right to him, snapped up a salute, and asked for what I wanted. I once got a furlough to go to see my people, and this made them good and sore. I wanted to see my people, and I didn't know what might happen to me once I got started to fighting. I had one sister that was awful mean, and I went to see her especially, because I did not know what might happen to her. She had an awful temper and was always in something. She jumped up one day and hung a cider bucket over the overseer's head because he tried to make her stop nursing the baby. The master came to her once to get after her for chopping another woman with a hoe. He told her he was going to send her to Mississippi. She right up and chopped him in the head with the hoe she was chopping with. "There now," he said, "she has done almost killed me." He didn't do anything with her about it. He wasn't so awful mean and didn't like to sell his slaves.

Some of them wouldn't stand for nobody to whip them. I helped to get a man's body who had drowned out of the river. He drew his wagon and team right in the river and drowned himself, almost drowned his master's team. His master was such a mean man and worked his slaves so hard that most of them either ran off or killed themselves. That is why I tell the youngsters of today that they don't know what we older people had to go through. We went through fire, and a hot one too. There wasn't no play about it. You had to do or die. Of course all the owners were not the same, but they were all mean and devilish enough.

After the war, times got worse for a time. The K.K.K. were raising the devil on every hand. They were especially hard on us soldiers. Once a bunch of them caught me out. "Where were you born?" they asked me. "Franklin," I replied. "You are the very Negro we want. You belong to that Union League, and we are going to kill you." "No sir, Mars's, I don't belong to no league, and I am a good man. I work for Ole Mars' and Missus and do whatever they tell me to." "You will have to prove this," they told me. They took me to a man that knew me, and he told them that I was once a soldier. This made them madder than ever. I denied that I had ever been a soldier, and when they tried to make me march I pretended not to know how. One of them stuck a pistol to my nose and asked me what church I belonged to. I said, "None." They told me I had better pray and made me get down on my knees. They had caught and killed a lot of Negroes that they found out to be old soldiers. I was good and scared. When I wouldn't pray, one of them started to praying for me and said, "Lord, have mercy on this poor Negro that is coming home in about five minutes." I jumped up and said, "White folks, I just can't stand it no longer." They jerked me around for a while and made like they were going to kill me, but after a while they let me go. I took off my hat and ran like a deer. It is a wonder I didn't run into a tree and kill myself.

I had some funny experiences during the war. One night I was on guard. I had stole a sack of roasting corn and had it hid near my beat. Now we were not supposed to fire our gun unless somebody failed to halt at command or tried to do some harm. I walked my beat a while, and after a while I stepped over to where I had left my sack of corn. When I got there I found that the 'coons had cut the sack and were destroying my roasting ears. I was so mad I lowered my gun and shot before I thought. The officer of the day came rushing out on his horse. "What is the trouble, Private? What is the trouble?" I knew I was in for hell if I didn't patch up an excuse and that mighty quick, so I said, "Sir, I saw something sneaking along in the bushes, and when I hollered at him to halt I shot at him." We searched around there for nearly an hour, trying to find out who it was. Of course we didn't find nobody, for there was nobody there. It saved me from a lot of punishment.

While I was on duty in Murfreesboro we used to have to bury a certain number of men every day. The burying ground was divided into sections, and we had to go out on the field, get our corpses, and bury them. Some nights me and my partner used to go out to the field and find two or three corpses that had been brought up by some of the others, take them to our grave, and bury them. In this way we would get through and be gone to Murfreesboro among the women before some of the rest got started. The old soldiers would have raised the devil with us if they had caught up with us stealing their bodies.

your sins all washed away

One night I went to the mourners' bench—I seemed to have the weight of the house on me—and I was in darkness. And whilst I was down on my knees I looked up, and I didn't see no housetop or sky. I just saw the clear heavens, and it looked milkish, and I said, "Lord, what is this?" And he said, "It is love." Then a shower of rain came down on the top of my head and went to the toes, and I was just as light as any feather, and I had on a long white robe, and I sailed and went upwards. Then I met a band of angels, angels who were praising God, and they looked at me and said, "Praise ye the Lord." The next morning I thought I didn't have any religion, and I heard a voice saying, "I have chosen you out of this world. Go tell the people what I've done for you." And I went in the house, and the voice came to me from the east singing:

> Your sins are all washed away,
> Free, free, my Lord.
> Your sins are all washed away,
> Free, free, my Lord.
> Your Father's done set you free.

When I was twelve years old I professed religion. One Sunday I began trembling like a leaf, and the tears were rolling down my face. For three days I couldn't eat or drink, and the white folks that owned me whipped me twice. I thought I would die. Then Jesus came to me just as white as dripping snow, with his hair parted in the middle just as white as snow. Then I was cut off like a streak of lightning. I didn't know nothing. I had never known anything about the Bible, but it was revealed to me. I was taught how to pray by the Lord. I belonged to the Kookler estate, and there were a hundred niggers on this estate.

I have had thirteen children.

One night I was carried off to a little white house by the Captain, and I heard singing, and there were a whole lot of little white children, and they were all bowing to me and singing welcome. The next morning my hands and feet were new. The Lord came to me when I was sick and told me that I was in the number that John saw.

A man once told me that he saw God as a natural man with a hickory shirt on and lying in a high feather bed.

before
the wind
ever
blew

I don't know why it was I got converted, because I had been doing nearly everything they told me I ought not to do. I danced, played cards, and done just like I wanted to do. I don't reckon I was so bad, but they said I was. In my heart I was good and felt that some day I would do better.

One day, when I was about twenty-two years old, I got up feeling awful heavy. I went about my work, and had started to washing when I suddenly began to feel worse and worse. I wasn't sick, I was just heavy. I began to say, "Lord, I wonder what is the matter with me?" I stopped washing and went in the house and layed across the bed, and there I saw Jesus. He turned my face to the east and said, "Go and declare my name to the world, and I will fill your heart with song."

While I was laying there I saw the city. It was the prettiest place that I ever saw. All the little angels were the same size and color, and as they flew, all their wings moved at the same time and made the sweetest music I ever heard.

After I passed through this experience I lost all worldly cares. The things I used to enjoy don't interest me now. I am a new creature in Jesus, the workmanship of his hand saved from the foundation of the world. I was a chosen vessel before the wind ever blew or before the sun ever shined.

Religion is not a work but a gift from God. We are saved by grace, and it is not of ourselves but the gift of God.

golden slippers on my feet

I was born in Williamson County and spent most of my life there. When I first heard the voice of God it was in broad daylight, and I was on my way home. A voice that seemed to ring through my soul said to me, "My little one, ain't you glad?" I was scared and started to run. The voice said again, "My little one, ain't you glad? Go and tell the world that you have found your Savior." I went home, that is, where I was working, but I didn't tell anyone about it.

I felt bad about it and got awfully heavy. About three days later, just as I was putting on some cabbage to cook for the farm hands, the voice said to me—it was so loud that it scared me and I thought surely the white woman heard it, for she was there in the kitchen with me, but on the other side of the room—"My little one, I have commanded you to go and you shall go. Behold, if you are ashamed of me I will be ashamed of you before my Father." I jumped and ran out of the kitchen crying, "Lord, have mercy! Lord, have mercy!" I was tearing my clothes and hair as I went. For two or three days I was like somebody foolish. I didn't know what I was doing half of the time.

I went to church on the Sunday following expecting to make a confession, but when I got there I wouldn't do it. About the middle of the preaching I was sitting looking at my ring on my hand. All at once it looked like something struck me on the top of the head and went on down to the sole of my feet. I fell to the floor. When I knew anything I was all dressed up in white. I had on a long white robe. I had on a golden belt about my waist and golden slippers on my feet.

I looked around me and saw hell and my old body black with smoke. On the inside I was crying, and a voice was saying, "Mercy! Mercy, Lord!" I looked and there stood a little man by me. He looked at me and said, "You have on your full armor. Follow me!" We were lost and got nearly to heaven when a voice said, "Amen!" Then I heard a shouting of voices saying, "Glory and honor to God forever." A voice said to me, "Go wash your feet and tell the world of my undying love. Amen."

everything just fits

I am now about sixty-seven years old. I was born in the year the Civil War started, in June. I had six brothers and seven sisters. My mother was a Baptist, and I often used to see her sit alone, knitting and singing. She would often get happy and shout. When she died I was only about ten years old. I used to hear her say, "I am so glad I am free." I did not know then what she was talking about. I thought she meant freedom from slavery.

I went to church and tried to get religion because I wanted to shout like Mama.

The first time I heard the voice I was in the cotton patch. A voice said, "Behold, I move you by the still waters." The voice was like muttering thunder. I kept on praying, and the next time I heard the voice it was many years later. I had married and had five children. I had been going to dances but continued always to feel the desire to pray. The voice said to me, "I am a spirit and am to be worshiped in spirit and truth."

The first time I ever saw a vision I saw myself a little body, pure white, and flying along a beautiful stream that flowed from the east.

Later I was chased by the devil. He chased me in a broad and rocky road, but he kept a good distance from me. I traveled in a western direction, but when my soul was freed I traveled eastward. I always prayed, and the prayer was on the inside crying, "Mercy, Lord!"

I still did not join church, and a little later I had my soul fixed up. I saw myself standing on a pretty white rock with nothing around it. I was afraid I was going to fall into the deep pit. It seemed that there was nothing to pity me. I was a little image, and my body was standing beside me. While I stood there, a little man came before me and said, "Don't you know that you will be devoured in here?" With this he took me in his arms and journeyed on a narrow white path that seemed no wider than a spider web. I saw three devils: one very large, one smaller, etc. They threw three large balls at me, and I cried and said, "Lord, if those balls should hit me they would tear me to pieces." We journeyed on and saw two lions lying by the side of the path. They were cream-colored. They did not move as we passed.

We journeyed on and came to a beautiful green pasture with beautiful green grass. Every sprig seemed even. There was a beautiful willow tree, and every limb seemed even. We came finally to heaven. My guide put me down and said, "I leave you in the hands of the mother." She arose—a very tall woman—and began to dress me. She had on a long white robe, and she dressed me the same way, and when she was through she said, "Everything just fits." I then began to shout and praise God with the rest of the angels.

We must see, feel, and hear something, for our God talks to his children. I joined the church after nearly ten years of experience, and I rejoice ever in the love of God. The love of God is beyond understanding. It makes you love everybody.

sixty-five years a washer and ironer

I was born in Robinson County. When the Civil War started, I was about twelve years old. My mother was the slave of an old man called Shaw. He was a Methodist preacher, but a mighty mean one. I wasn't hardly old enough to know much about him, but my mother told me how mean he was. He brought my mother here to Nashville and sold her when I was a little baby. After I got to be some size, my owner hired me out to some poor people that lived in the country. I was only about six years old, but I think he got about three dollars per month for me. They hired me to nurse, but I had to nurse, cook, work in the fields, chop wood, bring water, wash, iron, and in general just do everything. On Sundays they would go to church and leave me there to clean the house and cook dinner. There was no cooking stove, so I just had to use pots and kettles over the fire. For baking bread, I used a skillet and lid. This was done by putting hot coals on top of the lid. When they got back from church I always had the meal ready. If it wasn't ready, I knew what was coming. I didn't get many whippings, because I always did what I was told in a hurry. I hated to be whipped; I never got but one real hard whipping in my life, and that came from my mother. She put stripes on me from head to foot.

Every morning I was up at five o'clock. I slept in the room with the white folks. I made a pallet in the corner every night, and in the morning I took it up. After dressing myself, I made the fires, went and milked two cows, drove them to the pastures, and came back and brought water from the spring for the house. Then I cleaned up, helped with breakfast, and got ready to go to the field to work. The people who had hired me were poor, and they didn't have many people around to do the work, so I had to work awfully hard.

In the field my boss used to take two rows and give me one, and I had to be at the end with my one row when he finished his two. I knew what it meant if I wasn't there, so I usually kept up with him. I wasn't no more than eight or ten years old, but I could do as much work as a grown person.

While I was living with these people, I didn't see my mother more than once or twice a year. She usually managed to come to see me for Christmas week, and that was the last of it until maybe next Christmas. On some Sunday evenings I got a half an hour off to go to see some white people I knew. But as soon as the time was up, I had to go back to where I belonged.

When the Rebels and Yankees got to fighting around here, I ran off and came to Nashville to my mother. My mother sent a man for me one night, and we left for town about twelve o'clock. After we had gone some distance, the man showed me the way and left me. I went along half scared to death. All at once somebody said, "Halt! Who goes there?" I said, "Me." He asked me again who I was, and I just said, "Me." He told me to advance. I went up, and they got around me and asked me who I was and where I was going.

I told them that I had been working, and that I was trying to find my mother. I was cold, so they made a big fire and told me to sit there by the fire until day, because it would be dangerous for me to go on that night.

The next day they let me go on my way, and I found my mother. She hid me around until she got a chance to take me to a lady's house. All the slaves were running off about this time. I didn't know what the war was all about, but I used to hear the white people talking about the slaves getting ready to rise up against the white folks. It was dangerous for a slave to be caught out without a pass or something to show that his master knew where he was. Whenever the paddyrollers caught one, they almost whipped him to death. I used to hear the older people talking about freedom, but I didn't know what it meant. I hadn't done anything but work hard all my life. I didn't know how to read, write, or even spell my name. At the age of twelve, I was doing the work of a grown person. The people I lived with weren't so mean, but they kept me bowed down with work. They gave me the same food they ate. The other women on the place slept and ate in a big room, all together. I used to slip down where they were whenever I could find time. That is how I came to hear about the war and the coming freedom of the slaves.

I married when I was fourteen years old. I started to washing and ironing as soon as I came home to my mother, and I kept it up for sixty-five years. My mother was poor, but she was tidy and proud. She had a lot of Indian blood in her. She and my father didn't get on so well. I don't know why. She just said he wasn't right, and she didn't want to live with him.

I married a good man, and we lived together seventeen years and had six children. He died and left me with all those children to raise. He was a good husband and father and provided for his family as best as he could. He was older than I, and he used to tell me how to get along with my neighbors. He would say, "Now M., whenever your neighbors try to fuss with you, just keep your mouth; go in the house and shut the door and they will feel ashamed." Sure enough, I did this, and to this day I don't know that I have an enemy because I never quarreled with or talked about my neighbors.

After my husband died I had some hard times, but I had made up my mind to live right and bring up my children the best I could. On some days we wouldn't have enough food in the house for one to eat, but I would divide it among them. One day I was ironing, trying to get some clothes ready to send home. The children were all crying for food. I hated to borrow. I scraped up enough meal to make a little hoecake of bread. I broke it among them and went back to my ironing, crying. That day, about an hour later, some neighbor who cooked out came in to see me and brought me a little food she had put aside at the big house.

At this time, I didn't know anything about the Bible and God. I used to go along with the people that had hired me when I was a little girl, but I had to stay outside the church and take care of the baby. I was almost grown before I had ever heard the Bible read and the word of God explained. While a slave I didn't know anything but my earthly marster and mistress. We had to call them mars' and missey as soon as they were born, so I hadn't learnt anything about a heavenly Father and Marster of all. After I heard all these things, I joined the church. I cast my membership with the "Seventh Day Adventists" and stayed with them several years. I left them because I didn't believe in some of the things they taught. They didn't believe in eating meat, having pictures on the walls, or wearing any kind of jewelry. But whenever I wanted a piece of meat, I went ahead and ate it. One thing I did though that I have regretted ever since, and that was to sell the little jewelry my husband had given me. I still have faith in God, but not just as they taught it.

I managed to raise all my children and send them to school. They wore patched clothes, but they were clean. I taught them to keep clean rather than to have so many fine clothes.

I have lived to bury every one of my children, my mother, a grandchild, and every other earthly kin that I know anything about. I haven't any money, but I don't owe anybody a cent.

I live in a house that was bought by my son, but I may have to move at any time, for according to the deeds and papers it goes to his wife's people. I am a cripple with two sores on my feet that have been there for years and years, so I am not able to stand or walk very long. I did washing and ironing though, up until a few years ago when I got too weak to keep it up. I don't do anything now but sit around, entertaining my neighbors and making quilts. I have two very nice ladies that room here with me, and I live off of what they pay me for room rent. The neighbors come to see me and look after me. Whenever they don't see me out they always come around to find out the trouble. I sometimes think that my last days are to be my happiest days.

Last Christmas some young ladies from Fisk came down and brought me the nicest basket I ever saw. Oh! it made me feel so proud, proud to know that they would think of an old woman like me and bring me something. I bowed and thanked them the best I knew how. I have never had to ask the corporation for any help. One winter the Community Chest gave me some coal.

Times are better for the young people, and the old ones too, than they were when I was a girl. I was so glad to see the young people going to school and trying to learn something. My mother tried to make me go to school, but I wanted to work. I just felt like trying to make money. Too, I married early, and this killed my chances.

waiting for to carry me home

I was converted in Columbia fifty years ago and have been a member of the White Spring Baptist Church all this time. I was a slave and started to pray when I was nine years old. My mistress was mean to me, and one day she said, "I am going to kill you. Go and eat and come back to me, for I am going to kill you." I started out to eat, but when I got to the steps of the kitchen, I, a nine-year-old child, fell down and prayed to God saying, "Lord, I don't want to be killed. Save me." I went to the kitchen and ate nothing. I went back in the house, and she didn't touch me. From then on I prayed more and more.

Now I was a great dancer when I grew up, and in spite of my praying I went to dances. One night I went to a dance, but I didn't feel right and, strange to say, every time I got on the floor to dance a round, the fiddlestring would break. All of a sudden, while I was in my place ready to dance, I heard a voice on the inside that said, "Do you remember the promise you made to me?" I thought that everybody heard the voice; it was so loud. I ran out of the room and hid myself and started to praying. It was while praying that I died and found myself at the greedy jaws of hell. I saw the devil, a terrible, clubfooted man, with red eyes like fire. I called upon God to deliver me from that place, for the weeping and gnashing of teeth was awful. I saw a big wheel that seemed full of souls, and as it turned the cry of "Woe! Woe! Woe!" was pitiful.

All at once I felt myself lifted, and I came in the presence of God. A voice came to me saying, "My little one, I have given you eternal life. I looked upon you in the dust of the earth and blessed you with everlasting life. You are fixed and prefixed and bought at the lamb sale and caught up in the election and ready for the building."

I came to a building where I saw God. He sat writing, and without stopping he said to me, "I shod you with the gospel of peace at the greedy jaws of hell. Your name is written on the lamb book of life. Go back in yonder world and stay until I come, for when I come again it is without sin unto salvation." When he spoke those words, the whole place seemed to sound in a moan, "Amen." I looked about me and saw a green pasture filled with sheep, all pure white and of the same size.

I know my God and rejoice in him every day. Trusting him for my journey, I am not ashamed of his name or afraid of hellfire, for I have been killed dead and made alive again and am fireproof, rejoicing every day and waiting for him to carry me home.

angels
warm me
in my
dreams

When I was twelve years old I wanted to join church. My father told me that I had better not come home unless I seen something. When I joined I didn't see anything, and I was scared to go home, but just as I stepped out the door the heavens opened up, and I seed angels flying around. I ran to my father then.

One night I remember I was sick, and the doctors said I couldn't live. During this time I lay on the bed with my arms folded. To my mind, in the spirit, a little silver pipe was let down from the top of the ceiling, and three angels came down. On this little silver pipe I could hear their little wings flapping, click, click.

The doctors wouldn't allow me to eat. I'd be so hungry and thirsty, and these little angels would come down loaded with food. They gave me water out of the little silver pipe. I could feel each drop on my tongue. They told me this was the water of life. Some nights I'd be so cold, and they would huddle close to me and warm me in my dreams.

One day I told them I wanted to die. They told me to be ready the next time they came after me. And they came, but when they came three more came in front of them and told me that the good Lord wasn't ready for me. Then they flew up the pipe. As they reached the ceiling all six of them pulled the gates apart, and oh! how beautiful. I saw the souls of my friends lying under the altar.

I remember one night—oh, I used to love good times!—I was lying down after a dance. I felt so wicked. I laid and prayed, and while I lay there the prettiest music came to me. I told the Lord I wanted to see where the music came from, and I looked above me and saw many angels and heard the flapping of their wings.

I woke my children up to listen to the music. It was the prettiest I had ever heard. I wanted them to hear it.

I thought that night I was going to die.

i'll do
the separation
at the
last day

When Satan gets in the way he makes you say things you don't want to say. We all sin, and when the Lord started me out I prayed two or three weeks, and he freed my soul between week two and three. It was in the country. It was two or three in the morning. He came to me at the east part of the world and said, "Alice, you must die and go to hell this day." I fell down and said, "Have mercy on me." On the third day he came and repeated it. The last time, I put my sack off my back and got on my knees. Then a snake came and crawled around me, and then I went to the barn and leaned over a manger, and a cat came and brushed against me and scared me. I leaned over the corncrib, and the cat came again. I went on home and sat down on an old doorstep. Tears came from my eyes, and I cried, "Lord, have mercy, and what shall I do?" I fell over and hit the doorstep, and my mother came and picked me up.

He showed me all my dead sisters, and then he showed me all the angels huddled up and crowded around me. I was really soul-sick. A dove came and moaned three times at the foot of my bed. I sent for the deacon. I then seed myself baptized. The Lord was standing in the middle of the river and told me to follow him. He had a staff in his hand, and I was baptized in the water in Stone River.

I've been "perfessed" in 1902 on Thursday night. Sometimes I seen the sheep all in a green pasture. Some goats I seen too, and I heard my Master's voice saying, "Let the weak and strong grow up together. I will do the separation at the last day."

the sun in a cloudy sky

My religion is my life. It is the most important thing that I know now or that I will ever know.

I was born in Rockwood, Tennessee, and as a child I was taught certain religious principles. My father, who had some Indian blood, was a fiery preacher, and my mother was a very devout Christian. They would take me to church every day but, childlike, I could not enjoy the church meetings.

After I was fifteen they told me that I should get religion. I asked what that was, and they scolded me so greatly that I decided to try and get one. I thought one time that I had got religion, but I had not seen anything especial to convince them that I had been converted. I then prayed again and again but failed, that year, to get religion. When the next revival started I began at once to seek religion, and I found the Lord precious to my soul.

When I was converted I had gone about five days without eating, and I was in a graveyard by the side of my grand-father's tomb. There I heard a voice saying, "Rise, Mary." At first I decided not to rise, but then I heard the voice again, and all at once from a very cloudy sky came a beautiful sun. Then I jumped up and shouted to the Lord and started singing: "Give me that good old-time religion."

This I sang all the rest of the day, and I felt a burning in my heart, and a great burden seemed to have left me. I told my mother what had happened. She kissed me many times and told me that I had been converted, and I went my way rejoicing.

pray
a
little
harder

I am glad to talk to you about my religion, because it means more to me than I can express. I have been a member of the church for fifty-four years. I came through when you had to be a thoroughbred, and I mean I am a thoroughbred.

I was converted in a peculiar way, but I haven't got a peculiar religion. I have that kind that I am not afraid to express anywhere and at any time. I had to get down on my knees and stay there for several days, until the Lord freed my soul from the gates of hell. He did that because I asked him to show me my mother, who had been dead about twenty years. That he did. I asked him to protect me from evil spirits, and he did that. I remember one time when I was almost conjured by a hoodoo, and I prayed to the Lord and asked him to save me from him. I promised him if he would protect me and save me from being destroyed that way I would serve him the balance of my days. This he did, and I mean it has been a blessing.

I am a good old-time Christian. I have been serving the Lord for fifty years. I was converted in an old church out from the town of Columbia, Tennessee. I had to work hard to get my religion. I fasted and prayed for two weeks trying to seek the Lord. I was a great worldly person, and it was extremely hard for me to give up the ways of the world, but I had to come through right before I could be called a pure Christian.

The Lord has shown me many visions, and I know he lives true because he not only lives in my soul, as Job said, but he lives about me every day, and since I can't read he directs my path. When I was converted I lost sight of everything. While I was fasting I did not know where I was, nor did I know where I was going. One day about noon my mother came and found me, and it seemed as if I was afar off; but she kissed me many times and told me to keep on praying. I prayed and prayed and finally, after having many visions (some of them are so precious to me that I can't tell you), all of the evil things that I had done were shown to me.

I was carried to the very gates of hell, and the devil pulled out a book showing me the things which I had committed and that they were all true. My life as a midwife was shown to me, and I have certainly felt sorry, after I was converted, for all of the things I did.

When I testified in the church I had to tell all the things I had seen and heard. I heard one day, while I was out praying, a voice as if a mighty rumbling of thunder saying, "Mollie, Mollie, you must pray a little harder. You haven't come to the right place yet." I kept on until I asked the Lord, if he had converted me, to show me a beautiful star out of a cloudy sky. This was done, and I saw a star in the daytime shining out of a cloudy sky. I know I have got it, and hell and its forces can't make me turn back.

stayed with her people after freedom

I was born in Mississippi, in Juniper County. I belonged to Major Ellison, but I was raised right here in Tennessee till I was eleven year old; then Major Ellison bought me and carried me to Mississippi. I didn't want to go. They 'zamine you just like they do a horse; they look at your teeth, and pull your eyelids back and look at your eyes, and feel you just like you was a horse. He 'zamined me and said, "Where's your mother?" and I said, "I don't know where my mammy is, but I know her." He said, "Would you know your mammy if you saw her?" and I said, "Yes sir, I would know her. I don't know where she is, but I would know her." They had done sold her then. He said, "Do you want us to buy you?" and I said, "No, I don't want you to buy me. I want to stay here." He said, "We'll be nice to you and give you plenty to eat." I said, "No, you won't have much to eat. What do you have to eat?" and he said, "Lots of peas and cotton seed and things like that." But I said, "No, I'd rather stay here because I get plenty of pot likker and bread and buttermilk, and I don't want to go; I get plenty." I was staying with some half-strainers, and I didn't know that that wasn't lots to eat. He said, "Well, I have married your mistress, and she wants me to buy you"; but I still said, "I don't want to go." They had done sold my mother to Mr. Armstrong then. So he kept talking to me, and he said, "Don't you want to see your sister?" I said, "Yes, but I don't want to go there to see her." They had sold her to Mississippi before that, and I knowed she was there, but I didn't want to go.

I went on back home, and the next day the old white woman whipped me, and I said to myself, "I wish that old white man had bought me." I didn't know he had bought me anyhow, but soon they took my cotton dresses and put 'em in a box, and they combed my hair, and I heard them tell me that Mr. Ellison had done come after me, and he was in a buggy. I wanted to ride in the buggy, but I didn't want to go with him. When I saw him I had a bucket of water on my head, and I set it on the shelf and ran just as fast as I could for the woods. They caught me, and Aunt Bet said, "Honey, don't do that. Mr. Ellison done bought you, and you must go with him." She tied my clothes up in a bundle, and he had me sitting up in the buggy with him, and we started to his house here. I had to get down to open the gate, and when I got back up I got behind in the little seat for servants. He told me to come back and get inside, but I said I could ride behind up to the house; he let me stay there, but he kept watching me. He was scared I would run away because I had done run away that morning, but I wasn't going to run away, 'cause I wouldn't know which way to go after I got that far away.

When we got to the house, my mistress came out with a baby in her arms and said, "Well, here's my little nigger; shake hands with me." Then he come up and said, "Speak to your young mistress," and I said, "Where she at?" He said, "Right there," and pointed to the baby in my mistress' arms. I said, "No, I don't see no young mistress. That's a baby."

I went in the house, and they had all the glasses around there, and I just turned and looked and looked at myself 'cause I had never seen myself in a glass before. I heard Mistress say, "Po' little thing, she's just like a little motherless child; her mother was sold away from her when she was six years old." They had soft carpets, and I was just stepping and stamping up and down with my foot 'cause it was so soft, and then she took me up to a big room, and I said to myself, "Lord God, I got into another fine place!" The woman in there went in the trunk and got some domestic and some calico and made me a dress and some drawers and a drawer body.

She went to work and made those things for me, and then she told the women that it was time for her to go home, and she said take them duds and give them to your sister, and you comb her head and wash her all over. And, Honey, they washed me all over and put them things on me and I was never dressed so fine in my life. I just thought everybody was looking at me because I was dressed so fine. 'Course they wasn't paying me no mind a tall. The dress had some red in it, and some big flowers in it. I was looking at myself in the glass, and I would pull up my dress and look at my pretty, clean drawers and things, and when I went in the room where my mistress was I pulled it up again, and started looking and saying to myself, "Don't I look nice and clean under here?" and my mistress said, "You mustn't do that; that's ugly." Then I went out in the woods where there was lots of cedars thick around, and I got down there and pulled up my dress and just looked and danced and danced.

I had never been clean like that before, and staying with them po' white folks I had had a time with those body lice. They would get so bad I would take my dress off and rub it in the suds and rinse it out in the branch, and sometimes I would be rinsing it and mistress would call me. I would be so scared I would put it on wet and run to her. I had a time, I tell you. They might nigh eat me up when I was staying there, and I was so glad to be clean.

In the new home the overseer had a bullwhip, and Ole Marster had a strap, and I would hear them out in the field beating them and the slaves would be just crying, "Oh pray, Marster, oh pray, Marster." Ole Miss wouldn't let 'em whip me. She was just like a mammy to me. I wanted to die too when she died. Yes, she died right here in town. She called me in and told me, "Lu, I'm dying, but you be good to my chillen." And Mars' Tom would fan her, but she would always say, "Give it to Lu. You fan too hard, and I don't want you fanning the breath out of me; it's going fast enough without you fanning it away." I stood there and fanned her till she breathed her last, and then I ran in the next room and hugged my arms right 'round me and held my breath and tried my best to die. I was scared of him [Mr. Ellison] 'cause he cussed so much.

I stayed with my mistress while she was sick because they left Aunt Adeline up there to tend to her; and she tried to make her walk when she wasn't able to stand up, and I could lift her up in my arms. Mistress died on Saturday, and they buried her Sunday, and on Monday Mars' Tom called me and Aunt Adeline out and said one of us would have to go home [back to Mississippi], and the other could stay and take care of the chillen. I said right quick, "I'll go home," because I had a little boy down there I was crazy about, and I wanted to go back to him; but Marster got to crying and telling me that Mistress wanted me to stay with the chillen, and he said, "Stay with my little chillen and I'll never let you want. If you are a slave I'll take care of you, and if you are free you can always come to me and get what you need." So I stayed, and I had a hard time too. They just kept doing me so bad I started cussing. I said, "I'm getting goddamned tired of you knocking me 'round." There was one old woman [slave], and she just kept knocking on me and cussing me and calling me a goddamned yellow bitch, and she said she was gonna whip me that night if it was the last thing she did; and I told Mary Anne [slave] that "Ailee said she was gonna whip me if it was the last thing she did," and Mary Anne said, "If you let her whip you, I'm gonna whip you too." So that night I went to Hanna Bell and said, "Hanna Bell, hold my baby," and I give her my baby, and I come on down there where I knowed Ailee was gonna pass. I was kinder scared, but Hanna Bell said she would whip me too if I let her whip me, so I went on 'round. She come up and said, "You cussed me, didn't you?" and I said, "Yes, you cussed me too." And she jumped to me, and I just grabbed her round the waist and got straddle of her. Her sister come and looked on, but she didn't bother us, and I scratched her face and pulled her hair, and just beat her up terribly. Her other sister come and pulled me off her, and I started back at her. One of them run and told her husband, and he come running out and caught me by the arm; but I pulled my whole sleeve out of my dress and run back and hit her in the back.

Old Parks said he was gonna whip both of us when he found it out. When we went in the next day he saw my face where she had given me one scratch, and he said, "What on earth's the matter with you?" I told him that he had always told me to carry up the candle to put the chillen to bed, and Ailee whipped me 'cause I carried it up and didn't bring it back down; and she told him I cussed her, and that's why she hit me. He wanted to know if she cussed me too, and she didn't say nothing, and I said, "Yes, she called me a nasty, stinking, yellow bitch." He got up and boxed Ailee 'round scandless, but he didn't hit me but two licks. He never did hit me no more. He felt sorry for me 'cause I didn't have nobody to take up for me like the others.

I come up here the first year of the war, and I never did get back. No'm, he died down there [father of the girl].

I stayed with my white folks three years after freedom, and they tried to make me think I wasn't free; and I'll tell you I made it hot for them when they tried to bother the chillen [Master's children]. When he'd start to whip them I'd say, "You just let these chillen alone; Miss Janie [first wife] said you was gonna marry some other woman and be mean to her chillen," and he'd say, "Lu, don't tell me that," and I would say, "Yes, I is too, I'm gonna tell you every time you hit one of these chillen." One Sunday I wanted to go to a meeting in Franklin, and I didn't ask. I just told this woman I was going, and she said, "I say you can't go." I said, "Oh yes, I'm going," and she called Mars' Tom, and I told him I was going, and he said, "I say you can't go." So I said, "You look right here, Mars' Tom. I'm free, just as free as the birds in the air; you didn't tell me, but I know it," and he didn't say another word. You see, they thought that 'cause I stayed there I was fool enough not to know I was free, but I knowed it; and I went on to Franklin. I was nine miles from town, but I walked there to the meeting.

Later on they wanted me to go down to Mississippi to live, but I said, "I never spec' to go to Ole Sip again long as I live."

The chillen kissed me and told me goodbye, and they cried and cried. Later on he bought here, and they moved back, and I would go up there every month to see how my chillen was getting along. They would meet me down at a big tree and tell me, "She's [stepmother] just as mean to us as she can be," and they would take me up to the house and give me lots of things to carry home with me. I would tell Mars' Tom I come after some money and some clothes, too, and he'd give me a dollar and tell them to give me what I wanted; and they would go to the smokehouse and give me some meat and anything else I wanted. I still can get anything I want if I go to them, but it is hard for me to get way up there now.

[She was asked what became of the boy of whom she was fond.] He started up here, but the Yankees caught him and took him back. I never did see him no more.

I used to make the chillen cry during the war. I would say, "I'm going to the Yankees, Miss Maggie's getting just so mean to me," and the youngest child would say, "We'll go too. I'll tell you which a way to go." And she would a went with me too. All of them chillen would a went if I'd run away with them. I had a hard time, I tell you.

I married 'reckly after the war ceased. My old boss married his own niggers in Mississippi; he'd just get the Bible and marry them. He had the 'surance to marry me after the war, and he had to pay ten dollars for it too, cause he wasn't no officer that could marry me.

[In slavery time] they had a great big table set across the hall, and we would eat, and there was a place to dance, like we did on the fourth of July. We did have good things to eat on the fourth of July, and if there wasn't a fiddler on the place, Marster would hire one to come and play for 'em. That was in Mississippi, and down there they called us Tom Ellison's free niggers, 'cause he was better to us than most of them; but he didn't 'low no visiting. If you did any talking it was through the fence. You know white folks would just as soon kill you as not, and you had to do what they said.

They had a white man that would come over every fourth Sunday and preach to us. He would say, "Be honest, don't steal, and obey your marster and mistress." That was all the preaching we had down in Mississippi. They had benches and planks 'round for you to sit in, and a little table and a chair in the center for the preacher. When I'd come back from church they would ask how I liked it, and I would have to say I liked it fine. Your marster would whup you for going. You could go with the folks on your place but that was 'bout all.

When the war was coming up I would hear the white folks reading the papers about it, and I would run in the kitchen and tell Aunt Harriet. She would say, "Don't let the white folks hear you talk; they'll kill you." And if I would be going too far, she would stop me and wouldn't let me finish telling it to her.

Me and my sister was the brightest [in color] ones on our place. Yes, I got treated better'n any of them 'cause I stayed in the house, but sister had to work in the field, and she wasn't treated any better. They had an old woman to keep the colored chillen, and I would take my chillen [white] and go down to the quarters. I would stay down there and eat, and my chillen would eat down there too. Marster told Missie that that wasn't right, but we kept going, and he had to put out meal and meat for us down to the quarters.

He wasn't so mean, but the marsters cussed so much we was scared of 'em. One got to cussing 'round his little niggers, and they ran away. Some of 'em they never did find, 'cept their skeletons, where the varmints had destroyed 'em. They just found one over on a little island, and he had done stayed there so long when they found him he was right wild. They asked him what he had been eating after he got over it, and he said acorns and bugs and things like that. That man was neighbors to us, and our marster got scared then, and got good to his chillen. He had 'em up to the house once a week, and he would give 'em sugar and let them play up there and tell 'em they was his chillen and he wouldn't hurt 'em.

He was sorter mean, though, cause sometimes in the evening you would just hear that bullwhip crying. He'd tell the slaves to pick seven or eight pounds of cotton, and if they didn't do it he would whip 'em. He was so mean they got up a plot to run off, and they never come in till after twelve o'clock that night. They had plotted to go and jump in the Mississippi River and drown themselves; so after that he quit beating and knocking on 'em, and if he got an overseer that was too mean he would turn him off. They said they meant to drown, too, but they thought about their little chillen and come on home.

Yes, she is just fifteen years younger'n I am [daughter]. Her daddy died during the war. No'm, we didn't do much; just dancing and different kinds of plays. I et at the white folks house, and I et what they did, but he fed the others pretty well. He'd give 'em sugar and a peck of flour and coffee and things like that, and they could sell their part of the coffee if they didn't like it. He'd buy their winter clothes too. Everybody had two pairs of stockings and socks, and he didn't 'low 'em to work in the rain. He had two barrels of whiskey he kept in the smokehouse, and if they got a little wet they would have to come to the house and get a dram. He would tell 'em to come; and them niggers would get just a little damp, and they would come to the house and say, "Marster, I feel mighty cold and damp," and he'd get up and give them a dram. He got tired of that, so he bought some castor oil and would put that in the cup with the whiskey; but after while they would just drink it all down like they didn't care, and Mars' said he wasn't gonna let 'em drink his whiskey and his oil too, and he stopped putting it in there.

Yes, we had to have coffee and breakfast before we went to the field—just meat and bread. You couldn't have flour every day down there like they do here, you know. And talk about wild varmints! On a cloudy night you couldn't hear your ears for varmints. And you would see 'em drinking water at twelve o'clock in the day. And fish! You could catch 'em quicker'n you could run down a chicken and catch it.

I don't know nothing about my mother and father. She left us and run off. I was the oldest, and she left me and a little brother and another little suckling baby. She took us to the back porch at Morrisons and left us. On the way there she stopped at Aunt Jenny's and waited till nearly day, and then she took us and made a pallet on Morrison's porch and run away. She told us to lay there till she got back. I remember that Morrison come out of the door and asked me what we was doing there, and I told him Mammy told us to stay there till she got back, and he asked where she went, and I told him I didn't know. He went back and said to his wife, "Fannie, Ada's done run away, and her chillen's out on the front porch." Then he come back and told me to take the baby and my little brother and go 'round to the kitchen.

Mama, when she run away she stayed right here in town with old Carter for about a year. After she give him fifty dollars to keep him from telling on her, he 'trayed her; she found it out, and she left the barn where she was staying and come on back home. She seen old Carter pointing out the barn to a nigger trader, and she left there. Old Morrison kept her 'bout two weeks after she come back; then a nigger trader come long, and he sold her. He said it was no good for him to keep her, 'cause if he'd hire her out she would whip the white folks. She had a scar right up over her eye, and she got it fighting white folks. I remember it 'cause I remember getting slapped about picking at it when I was little. She would chip 'em and strip 'em naked and carry 'em up to the courthouse where Marster was.

We was raised up without a mother, and one old woman in the house where we stayed was so mean to us she would take nettle weeds and whip us with 'em. [This was prior to her trip to Mississippi.] I had to get up and go to the spring and get water and come back and take breakfast. Charlie [brother] was sick, and we took him out in the yard and let him set up so he could see us play, and after a little while he said, "I want to lay down; I'm tired of sitting up." I took him and laid him down, and just then they called me to the house to get some eggs to make egg bread. After I got 'em I slipped back down to see how he was, and I called him and he wouldn't answer, and I pulled his eyes open and he didn't say nothing, and I flew up to the kitchen to Aunt Bet [cook] and told her, "Aunt Bet, Charlie's gone to sleep, and I can't wake him up." She went over, and he was dead.

Charlotte, the old woman we was living with, was mean to us. She would make the little one [Tobe] get up and go outdoors to do his business [body functions], and he would stay out there till I'd come and get him and bring him his breakfast. I would dip my hand in the gravy and rub it on his toes when his feet was cold. One morning I brought his breakfast, and he couldn't eat, and I tried to open his mouth, and I couldn't, so I took it to Aunt Bet. She was my friend. I said, "Tobe can't eat; he can't open his mouth," and she come back with me. Tobe was sitting there and had lockjaw, so she had to go to the white folks. They sent for the doctor, but he couldn't do no good; he stayed all that day, but the next night Tobe died. They made me go to the spring to get some water to bathe that child, and it was so dark I couldn't see my hand before my face. When I got back with the water, Tobe was dead; so I didn't get to see neither one of my brothers die. If I live to see this coming March I'll be eighty-nine years old. I can't see and hear so well now. No'm, the girl's father died [her daughter's father]. I didn't know my brothers' daddy at all, but they said his name was Riley, and that they named Tobe Riley after his daddy. He was the darkest child Mammy had.

I'd go down to my sister's house and do my courting down there. I could go down there and stay till nine o'clock. Marster would make his slaves marry who he wanted 'em to marry. You couldn't marry who you wanted to. That was here, when my brothers died. Mama said she could tell when her chillen died. When every one of them died she said her nose would drop a drop of blood; and she said when the two boys died she went over to a neighbor's house and told her that they was dead 'cause her nose dropped a drop of blood. When she come back after freedom she was here in town a week before I knowed it. I had just had a fight with my husband, and I had just told him that if I had a mammy to go to I would leave and never come back to him. That night we had gone to bed, and it was raining real hard, and I heard somebody holler and thought it was somebody coming for him to hunt. He said they could just holler on then, but that was my mother and my little half-brother there. It was dark, and they was at the river and couldn't find the footlog. They finally found somebody and asked them how far it was to Mr. Mayberry's place, but when she got there they told her it was back the way she come, and to go to some of the colored folks' house and stay till morning and get an early start. She went and knocked on a door, but just as soon as she did they all put out the lights, and nobody wouldn't come to the door. So she went back to the white man's barn and got in the hay and stayed all night. In the morning she got up and come walking up to my house in the rain. It was in February. She walked up to the door. I had two little girls and was whipping one of them when the woman come to the door and asked who lived there. I told her Kay Mayberry lived here, and I'm his wife. So she said, "You don't know me?" And I said, "No'm, I don't believe I made your acquaintance before, but come in out of the rain." And she come in and asked me again if I knowed her, and she stepped over to the door. But I didn't know her, and the boy said, "This is your mother, and I'm your brother." I said, "No, my mother's sold and my brothers are dead." I said, "You're none of my mammy. I know my mammy." Then she took the bundle off her head and took off her hat, and I saw that scar on her face. Child, I look like I had wings! I hollered for everybody. I 'larmed out all the neighbors, and it was just like the "sociation" 'round there. She stayed with us a long time, and she died right here in this house.

[Courting] We would just sit and talk with each other. I told him one time I didn't love him, I hated him; and then I told him again that I loved him so much I just loved to see him walk. You had to court right there on the place; 'cause they had paddyrollers, and if you went out without a pass they would whip you.

there ain't no conjurers

I am a great Christian. When I was converted I passed through many ordeals. I was a person who did not want to give up all of the worldly things, although I wanted to be a good Christian. I loved to drink, and I loved to play the fiddle, and I don't believe anyone can be a good, devout Christian and do these things.

It took me about three weeks to "come through" with my religion. If I had not been a lover of those worldly things, it would not have taken me so long. I prayed every day all day long, in a big, open field that was just being opened up as new ground, for three weeks. When I was out there neither did I eat a thing nor drink more than a little water. This seems strange to you, but for three weeks I ate only four pones of bread about the size of your hand. I was full up to my throat, and I did not want anything to eat. After my conversion I was happy, and I spent a whole week going over the community, telling everybody what happened to me. I was the happiest person in the whole world. I have gone on praising the Lord since that time.

I have seen many visions. This is why I believe in God more strongly. Everything I have asked him to show me he has shown. I remember once I asked him, about midnight, to show me my dead mother and father, and he did that. He has shown me the way to go all through life. When I get mixed up in life, he will show me the way out. I believe in my God because he will reveal things to one who is devout and one who does his bidding. I can tell nearly every time just how long a person is going to prosper. I can tell when evil is upon a person. This is something that I think the Lord will do for anyone who is devout.

I don't believe in conjurers, because I have asked God to show me such things—if they existed—and he came to me in person while I was in a trance and said, "There ain't no such thing as conjurers." I believe in root doctors because, after all, we must depend upon some form of root or weed to cure the sick.

felt
the darkness
with
my hands

Jesus called my attention to a clock.

I was at the church one night, and there was a fellow who preached a sermon comparing a man with a clock. That is: a clock will run and run and stop; then you will carry it to the jewelry shop and have it repaired from time to time; then, after a while, you will take the clock and throw it in the trash basket. The same with a sinner.

One night I got sick, and I wasn't sick somehow. Well, anyway, there was something that happened to me. I couldn't sleep, and it went on this way for a week or more. I would take a drink of water and couldn't swallow it; it would swell up in my throat.

One night, while I was going to church, something began talking to me. It was a sort of prayer, and the voice was crying, "Mercy, Lord." And when I got to Warner Street I loses sight on this world, and I run into Mount Olive church door, and they tell me that I run over a red-hot stove. I went in praising God.

The next morning on going to work I meets a woman, and she told me to talk to her about my religion. But Jesus hadn't talked to me, so I decided to ask him to talk to me. I turned around and went back home and pulls off my pants and lays them and myself across the bed and puts my hand on my feet and said, "Lord, show me some sign that I am your child."

Immediately I wheels over on my back and throws my eyes in the east corner of my house, and I spied a white man through the eye of faith. And when I looked again I could see the "Boss" plain, and he was hanging up on the cloud, and a white girdle come across his shoulder and crossed under his arm, and the wind had it shivering. He held his hand up to me, and I could see the gash in his hand. And he talked to me and called me his little one, and his voice was so powerful it hit me in the top of my head and stood me up on my feet. I went all around the square in my underclothes.

I asked the Lord to show me whether I was his child again, and he showed me myself in two parts of me. He carried me off in the spirit, and showed me this old body in the ground and my new body up in the air and me singing, "Hark from the tune."

The next time I told him I wanted to see hell, and he carried me through hell, and I saw a lot of people hanging on a big wheel; and they had rags on their heads, and the wheel was going over and over, and every time it went over you could hear the groans of the people, and it was dark. I could feel the darkness with my hands. Then Jesus talked to me.

I asked him the next time to show me heaven, and so one night he showed me the sinner's path. I was going some place, and the devil got after me and carried me down a big, broad street. He was on a big, black horse running me for life and death, and he was jumping after me with a pronged fork. Suddenly I saw a path no larger than a pencil, and I went down that and looked around, and the devil was standing there shaking his head as if to say, "I'll get you next time." When I reached the end of the path I came to a little white house, and a little white man was there to welcome me, and it was all lit up with twelve candles.

One night when I was coming home about something after eleven, something happened to me. I had always craved to have a deal to say. And so I worried over it for a long time. One night I was coming by the capitol uptown, and I heard a voice ringing in my ears, "Behold." I looked around and saw nobody, and so I began walking faster, and the voice spoke again, "Behold." And there wasn't a soul around but me, and it said again, "Behold the stars." I looked up, and the voice came from heaven and said, "There are little stars and big stars." God was showing me that there were big Christians and little Christians.

When I was ill I was dying for three weeks. I was so heavy with sin I was heavy as lead, and when my sin came off it fell in hell, and I could see the sparks fly up higher than I could see where it fell. The trees bowed to me and said, "Good morning, sir."

One time God told me, "To all of my sheep I give a stone, and only those that receive it can read it. The stone is this: the seal of grace. Nobody can talk about the religion of God unless they've had a religious experience in it." He told me, "My little one, all of my sheep have a well of water," meaning this: You have noticed some people get happy and cry, and the tears are the well of water.

jesus
handed
me
a ticket

Before I begin I want to say that I don't know what other people have heard and seen in the spirit, nor do I know whether it is necessary for everybody to see and hear what I have experienced, for God knows what is best. It may be that some people do not need to see or hear anything. I say this because I do not want anyone to feel that I think God deals with everybody in the same way. The secret is with him, and he reveals things to whomever he wills and as he wills.

My first experience came one night just after I had gone to bed. I was twelve years old at the time, and it had never occurred to me that I had to die. In fact, I had never given it a thought until that night. I was not asleep but had just closed my eyes when I saw, in a vision, a beautiful little white chariot floating through the air; and I was in it. There was no one with me nor was I guiding the chariot, but it just went along sailing through the air. In time it passed through a dark tunnel or dungeon, and here I saw a lot of devils. They all seemed to be working, but as I passed through they stopped and threw things at me. I sailed on unafraid.

After some time I came to heaven. I saw God sitting in a large armchair, his head up and looking into space. He neither moved nor spoke. He wore a full armor, and across his chest was a breast-protector that shone as if it was made of bars of gold. My mother was standing there, and she showed me my two brothers who had died. I looked around and saw hosts of angels around two long tables, and they were shouting and clapping their hands. The tables were covered with white cloth that hung evenly all around and nearly touched the ground, which was covered with beautiful green grass. The angels would come up to the table, take one mouthful of food, and go away shouting and rejoicing, saying, "Praise God!"

From this time on I was made to know that I had to die. On another night, not long afterwards, I saw my two oldest brothers sailing through the air and going towards the east. The younger brother was in front. I did not know at that time what it meant, but about five years ago I lost the younger of the two brothers, and two years later the older one died.

A few years after I saw my first vision I became sick and was tormented by old Satan nearly every day. I seemed to be looking through the wall of my room into a large ballroom where dancing and all kinds of amusements were going on. The devil would seem to come in my room and make faces at me and beckon me to the ballroom. How he entered my room I don't know, but he would suddenly appear before me with his claw-like hand, beckon to me, and then enter the other room. He kept worrying me until I decided to pray.

One day, while lying there in bed, I saw a star. It came and rested right on the window sash, where the pieces that hold the panes of glass cross one another. I looked through that star and saw the heavens open, and a sword came out and was laid on my bed beside me. A voice said to me, "When Satan comes, show him this sword." The devil came back and started towards me, but when he saw the sword he vanished, and I never saw him again.

At another time something that looked like a blackboard flashed before my eyes, and on it were my sins. There was no writing, but I was made to know that they were my sins. A voice said, "Though your sins be as scarlet, I will wash you as white as snow; though they be heaped up like a mountain, I will roll them away as a scroll."

When I was about eighteen years old I began to think seriously about the salvation of my soul, and I began to pray saying, "Lord, show me if I am right." Not long after this I saw in a vision three heads side by side, one just a little above the other—the Father, the Son, and the Holy Ghost. A voice spoke to me and said, "My little one, thy faith hath made thee whole. Amen." I shouted for joy.

Once again I saw, as it were, a ladder. It was more like a pole with rungs on it let down from heaven, and it reached from heaven to earth. I was on the bottom rung, and somebody was on every rung, climbing upward, but no one seemed to be in a hurry.

Once I saw two men. I was made to know that one of them was Jesus, and I wanted to speak to him. I hurriedly came up to him, but I was ashamed for I wanted to speak to him privately. While I stood hesitating, another man came up in great haste and handed a ticket through the window and passed out to a platform to take a train. My knees got weak, and I knelt to pray. As I knelt Jesus handed me a ticket. It was all signed with my name. I arose to my feet and handed it in at the window and was told to take my place with the three men standing on the platform and wait.

One other time I saw Jesus in a vision, and this time it was a warning of death. I saw in the west one evening a cloud, and in it I first saw a man's foot, but as I looked I saw the head exposed at another point in the cloud. I began to cry and shout for joy because, for some reason, I was made to feel glad. About a month after this a very dear uncle of mine died, and I think that this vision was a warning.

This is the way the Lord has dealt with me. Seldom does anything happen in my family but that I get a warning.

God knows what he is about, and the best that any of us can do is to follow as he directs us through the spirit.

What is good for one person may not be suitable for another. God is the judge.

little me
looks
at old,
dead me

One night, after I had made many promises to the Lord and broke them, a voice said to me, "You remember the promises you made to me while in the country?" I became worried. I was working in a lumberyard. One day I just seemed to get blind, for every time I would try to put down a piece of lumber I would let it fall on my feet. I began to cry and whisper to the Lord. When time came to eat I couldn't eat, for the food seemed to cry, "Unworthy." Sometimes in the middle of the night I would find myself on my knees praying. I couldn't rest. I was not a believer in revivals, because I didn't feel that any man had any more than I did.

On another night the voice said again, "Remember the promise you made to me while in the country." A few nights later I was persuaded to go to a revival. I went up front and heard the preaching. The voice on the inside began to cry, "You got to die and can't live."

I died and saw a deep hole, and a little man called to me saying, "Follow me." I journeyed on and came in sight of a beautiful green pasture and a beautiful mansion. There were sheep, and they were all the same size. I don't know how I left, but I do know how I went to heaven. I declare to you I saw myself in two bodies. Little me was standing looking down on the old, dead me lying on a cooling board. While I was in the mansion I saw a beautiful white bed, and one man came and made it for me and turned and said to me, "That is yours."

I am not hell-scared or devil-dodging, for I know that I have died and don't have to die anymore.

barked
at
by the
hellhounds

I was fifty-two years old when the Lord freed my soul. About three years before I was killed dead and made alive again. I was feeding some hogs and was in the pigpen when a little white man appeared before me as plain as day and said, "Follow me." How it happened I don't know, but I do know this: I crossed Fountain Creek in the spirit, and I walked on top of the water. Something on the inside of me began to cry, "Mercy!" The little man said to me, "You have but little faith. Follow me in the spirit, and I will strengthen your faith. Believe in me with your heart, and I will show you many wondrous things."

We journeyed east and saw the heavens and God. Jesus Christ himself brought me to Fountain Creek Church and said, "This is your home."

During the vision the voice first said to me, "Here you must die." I truly died and saw my body. I had a temporal and a spiritual body. My spiritual body had six wings on it, and when I was barked at by the hellhounds of the devil I arose and flew away.

Ever since the Lord freed my soul I have been a new man. I trust in him to fight my battles, for he is a captain who has never lost a battle or been confounded with cares. I am always glad to meet those born of God, for I can feel the pull.

behold, i am a doctor

I am now sixty years old and was born in Georgia.

During my young life I was about like most of the boys—thinking and fooling around and idling away my time. When I was about twenty-two years old I got sick, and I remember that then I began to feel bad because of the life I was leading. I thought about the Lord and began to pray to him to forgive me for my sins.

One day, after I had taken a lot of medicine and had about everything the doctors could give me, I remember lying on my back looking up at the ceiling. Of a sudden I saw beyond the ceiling and seemed to see the heavens open and a hand come forth which hit me in my face, while a voice said to me as loud as thunder, "I am a doctor." That very minute I seemed to get stronger. I got well a little later. I thought about the voice I heard for a long time, but then again I forgot God and started to doing like I had been doing all my life.

A long time after the first spell I got sick again, and this time I was so sick that I would not move my hands or feet. In whatever way they placed me, there I stayed until somebody turned me over. Again I prayed and told God how I had not done what I had promised. One day while I was very sick and weaker than usual I saw the heavens open, and the same voice said to me, "If you are sick, behold, I am a doctor!" At the same time the hand came forth and seemed to slap me in my face. Until that minute I had not been able to raise my hand, but immediately I gained strength, and in less than five minutes I felt strong enough to get up, dress, and go out. From this time on I promised to serve the Lord and try to become a Christian.

I went to church very much and prayed every day. I didn't say much when I prayed. I just asked the Lord to have mercy on me because I felt sinful, and I always asked him to teach me how to pray and to save my soul from a burning hell.

One Sunday night after I had got back home from church I got to feeling very glad. I walked to the bed where my wife and little daughter were sleeping and kissed them. I walked the floor, crying and wringing my hands. I don't know why I was crying. I just felt so good.

I went to bed, and—I remember as well as if it had happened yesterday—I heard the clock strike for midnight. My eyes were wide open, and I saw heaven spread out before me. It was so bright up there that I couldn't look at it. Then a voice like thunder, but calm, said to me, "My little one, weep not, for lo! I have heard your prayers, and I am come to deliver your soul from the jaws of hell and place your feet on the eternal rock. Rejoice and be glad, for lo! all your days I will have mercy on you." Then I saw a hand come forth out of heaven, and I died. The voice said to me again, "I have unstopped your deaf ears, cut loose your stammering tongue, and opened your blinded eyes. Fear not, for you are a chosen vessel, and many shall hear your testimony and believe on my name."

When he said that—God bless your soul—I felt his power. It was like lightning; it came so quick I was killed dead. The next thing I remember was that I was standing on the brink of hell. I was in two bodies: there was a little William and the old William. Little William stood looking down on old William, my earthly body. I got scared and started to praying, "Lord, have mercy!" I said this because I saw my old body lying at hell's dark door. Quicker than a flash I was caused to turn away by the power of God, and looking in the east direction, I saw a little white path. It was very narrow, but straight. The voice said to me again, "My little one, I place your feet in the straight and narrow path. Be not afraid, for I will be on your right hand and on your left. I will be as a refuge and a fortress. Wherever you go let this be your testimony, for I am with you always, even until the world shall end. Amen." Then I heard the heavenly host sing the "Canaan, Fair and

Happy Land, Where My Possessions Lie." It was the prettiest song I ever heard. I came back to myself as the clock struck one. I was shouting and crying all night; I was so glad. Glad to know that I had waited at hell's dark door and got my orders to travel. I have been traveling ever since, looking to my Captain for my every want and need.

slavery was hell without fires

I was born in Franklin, long before the Civil War. I belonged to the family of B. While I was little I did about everything but say my prayers. I was born in a little log cabin in the cabin lot. This was a place fenced off and filled with cabins for the slaves. My mother was the mother of nineteen children. I have one brother and two sisters living. Most of them died before I came along, so I never saw many of them. We were all brought up together. My mother used to pray and sing and shout all the time.

Before the war my father was sold and carried away. While he was away he married again. After the war he came back and wanted to come back to Mama, but she told him no and said for him to stay with the woman he had. But he left her and took another woman and went to Mississippi.

My master gave my mother and us children to his son, and he took us to Culleoka. But during the war my father came there and got us and brought us to Nashville and put us in the Capitol, where we would be fed and taken care of.

When I was little I used to work around the big house, cleaning floors, polishing silver, wiping floors, waiting on the table, and everything. My mother was the cook. My mistress was awful mean and exacting. I had better not do anything wrong. She used to beat me like I was a dog—hit me across the head with tongs or poker or anything. There were some wooden steps in the hall leading upstairs. One day I was going up them, and she got mad because the steps creaked. She hollered at me and called me to her and said, "You black bitch, you go up those steps like a horse. I'll kill you." Hardly a day passed that she didn't beat me for something.

When we were coming from Culleoka, my mother nearly knocked all my teeth out bumping my head against the floor. They were having a scrimmage, and the troopers came by and hollered, "Lay down! Lay down! Lay down!" I wanted to see, so I kept raising up to see what was happening. My mother would push my head down against the floor of the car.

When we got to the Capitol it was just packed with women and children, both white and colored. We were all huddled there together, slept together and ate together, and there was no distinction either in the food we received or the care we got. We all had to stay inside until the fighting was over.

Sometimes, when my mistress would beat me over the head, Mars' Bill used to call me to him and look at my head and say, "May, what is the matter with your head?" I would tell him then, and he would scold my mistress.

Sometimes she used to suffer with yellow jaundice, and the doctor would put her in a tub and pour water over her. I would have to run back and forth to the spring to bring her water, and didn't make no difference how quick I went and came, nor how sick she was, she would fuss and call me a black, nappy-head bitch and try to hit me.

Sometimes when the snow was on the ground my mother used to stand at the cellar door to slip me a pair of dry moccasins to put on. My feet were so frostbitten that you could track me everywhere I went through the snow. When I think back over what I came through I wonder that I am still living or that I didn't lose my mind. I was beat over the head and knocked around so much that my head and back stayed sore all the time.

I used to see haunts when I was young. One day I was coming from the spring and had a bucket of water on my head and two buckets in my hands when I came up to the door. It was in the evening, and Mars' B. had been dead over a year. I looked up as I started up the steps, and there I saw his ghost. It was exactly like him, standing leaning against the side of the door with his red handkerchief around his neck and his legs crossed. He was looking across the pasture towards the big hill. I said, "Mars' Bill." He didn't move or speak but just stood looking up the hill, as he did every day while he was living to call the hogs. I just stooped and went under his arm. When I went in Mistress said, "Who was that you were talking to? Hush, you black liar. I heard you calling Mars' Bill, you black, kinky-haired bitch. I will kill you." With that she struck me and almost beat me to death.

One other time I saw him. It was one night while I was carrying supper to the cabin lot, to Mama. I heard something walking behind me, and when I looked around I saw Mars' Bill, a great, tall man nearly as tall as a tree. Usually I wasn't scared of him, because I was his pet in his lifetime, and he used to keep mistress from whipping me. But when I looked up at him and saw that he didn't have any head on it nearly scared me to death. He was all dressed up in a black coat and pants and white shirt, but he didn't have no head. His hat was on his neck. He was right on me when I looked up and saw him, and I ran through him, breaking off the latch and falling in the door where Mama was lying sick. I didn't spill her supper, but the pan slipped out of my grip and slid under her bed. Some of them heard me hollering and came to see what the trouble was. They picked me up and laid me on the bed, but it was some time before I got over the scare enough to tell them what I had seen.

When my mistress heard about it the next day, she beat me again. "You black, ugly, snotty-nosed bitch, I will teach you to be going around here talking about seeing your Mars' Bill." But in spite of her beatings I still stuck to it that I did see him.

Not long after this she saw him, and he like to have scared her to death. She was sitting in the room alone by the fire when he appeared before her, and such hollering you never heard. When I went in to find out the trouble, she tried to make believe that a big rat scared her. She said this because she didn't want me to know that she had seen him. But she got so nervous that she was afraid to stay in the house. I guessed what the trouble was even before it got to be hinted around that his spirit was coming back tormenting her. She beat me for saying that I had seen him, and my God was just causing her to suffer for her meanness. She lived until after the war. I heard of her before she died. She went out of this world just like she lived—fussing and cursing.

I used to see haunts so much I prayed to God that I might not see any more. And I don't see them now like I did then, since I became an elect in the house of God. He has taken fear out of me. He shows me things, but they are spiritual and come from his matchless wisdom, and the world can't see nor understand them. I profess to know nothing about the world nor its ways. I can't read a line either of the scriptures or any other kind of writing, but I do know this: Whenever the truth from heaven is read before me I can talk to the Father. Others may read and talk, but I go to the telephone that is always in operation and ask the Father, who is never too busy to answer. So I may not speak the words just like they are in his printed book, but I am right anyhow and know it. I often wish I did know how to read, but since I didn't have the chance to learn—being fearsome to be seen with a book when I was a slave—God has seen my need and made me satisfied. He has taken me, a fool—for sometimes my head was beat so I thought I was foolish—and hidden with me the secret of eternal life. He has made me to stand up on my feet and teach the world-wise out of his wisdom that comes from on high.

Sometimes I am caused to feel sad because I see people going around telling lies and talking about religion when I know they don't know what they are talking about. When such people come around me, I usually go to God and say, "Lord, am I right?" And he never leaves me in ignorance. Neither does he leave any that trust him in ignorance. The soul that trusts in God need never stumble nor fall, because God, being all-wise and seeing and knowing all things, having looked down through time before time, foresaw every creeping thing and poured out his spirit on the earth. The earth brought forth her fruits in due season. In the very beginning every race and every creature was in the mind of God, and we are here, not ahead of time, not behind time, but just on time. It was time that brought us here, and time will carry us away.

I know nothing about what God said to the prophets of old, but I do know what he has said to me. And I know that I have a counselor in him that never fails. When danger comes, he works on my mind and conscience and causes me to walk around the snares set for me by my enemies. What earthly friend could do this? Why, the latter would say, "I would have warned you, but I didn't know there was danger ahead." That is why I trust in God, because he sees and knows all things. And because I trust in God, he leads me into all wisdom and shows me the failings of hypocrites and liars.

Not many years ago my daughter had a very dear friend named J. She was a good woman and worked hard all the time and always kept herself neat and clean, but she was a great lover of money. Oh! she was just money-crazy! One day while I was in bed sick she came in to see E. and me. I said, "I am not much today, J.; how are you?" She complained of being sick. When she said that it just looked like sorrow filled my heart. I was weak, but I raised myself to a sitting position in the bed and began to talk to her. I was always after her about her ways and telling her she ought to try to pray, and my daughter used to tell me I shouldn't be so hard on her; but I kept it up. On this particular day I felt more bold than usual, and I couldn't hold my peace. She was sitting before the fire with her elbows on her knees and her head resting between her hands. I said, "J., you ought to pray, because you are not going to be here always." She said, "Oh, Mama, I do pray." I said, "J., you have never prayed a heartfelt prayer in your life. So hush and don't say no more, for you are just lying." She didn't get mad but just sat there, and I saw the tears rolling down her cheeks. She got up after a while and said she was going to get her money. She did washing and cleaning for some people who kept a restaurant. I said, "J., you had better not go there today because you know how you are; you will start to working and dabbling in water, and it won't be good for you." "But I want my money, Mama," she said. I told her she had better just go on to the drugstore and get some medicine and let that work and money alone. Too, I told her, Miss R. will pay you, and she won't mind if you don't wash today.

While she was still sitting there, S., a cousin of mine, came in and spoke and sat down by the fire. Everything got still for a few minutes, and I raised up in the bed. I was still feeling worried and sad about something. When I looked I saw J. pointing at S.'s legs and laughing, making fun of her because her legs were so little and skinny. My soul caught on fire. The child looked so tired and sad. I broke loose like a storm because I couldn't help it. I said, "Oh J., mark you, I see you laughing at that child. You had better be praying. The same power that keeps her alive has your destiny in his hands. When death comes, what difference does it make how you look? That child will be here long after your grave has become level with the ground. You had better set your heart right with God, because he is going to visit you before long." I said all this to her and more. I kept telling her she had better try to pray.

After a while she got up and told me goodbye and said she was going after her money. I said, "All right, Honey, but don't do any work because you are not able." That evening late she came back by to see me and said, "Mama, I got my money and didn't do anything but wash off a bedstead, and now I am going to the drugstore and buy some medicine."

That night she took some of the medicine, bathed her feet, and went to bed as the drugstore man told her to do, but she didn't seem to get any better. Now J. had a very wild daughter, and she didn't like her very much because she was so reckless and was always causing her mother so much trouble. She bought some wash-medicine from the drugstore. It was deadly poisonous and not to be even put near the mouth, but through some accident or other this daughter gave J. some of this poison dose. In a little while she got very sick and couldn't speak. They called for E., my daughter, to come over, and she got two or three other women to go with her. They called the doctor right away, for J. was sinking fast. The doctor came, and I saw right away what her trouble was. He gave her a shot in the arm and told them to leave her quiet until ten o'clock. He knew she would be dead, but he just told them that. My daughter had been with her all night, and about seven o'clock she came back and told me that J. was awful sick. I wanted to go and see her, but I couldn't. I just turned over in bed and got awful sorrowful and heavy, and then, all at once, the burden seemed to be lifted. E. had gone back and left me then by myself. A few minutes after she left me, I saw, in a trance, myself lying across my bed, and it seemed that I was looking out across a place filled with bushes and logs. I was elevated up and was looking out across this place, and the first thing that caught my eye was a tall man, standing off at a great distance on a log with his head thrown high. He was looking at me as if he was trying to pierce me through with his gaze, and my eyes seemed glued on him. While I was still gazing at him and he at me, a woman appeared. Before I saw her, she called to me three times in a soft, sorrowful voice. She had her arms folded and came up on the right of the man that was staring at me. Just before she passed on behind him, she looked up and moaned, "Oh, Mama; oh, Mama; oh, Mama!" It was so pitiful that my very heart looked like it would melt in me. But I kept my eyes fixed on that strange-looking, tall man, and he never once took his eyes off me. She passed on behind him and looked up at me and said, "You are in the yard, stay in the yard; you are hidden in the yard, and they can't find you." When she said this she passed on and entered a door, and when she opened the door, screaming and arguing and fussing such as I had never heard came from the inside of that place. After she went in and closed the door, the noise gradually died out of my ears, and I came back to myself again. I said, "Lord, have mercy! Lord, have mercy! J. has gone into such a place as that. Lord, have mercy! Lord, have mercy!"

In a few minutes, E. came running and said, "Oh Mama, J. is dead." I said, "Yes, Honey, I know it. She came by and told me goodbye." She said, "Oh Mama, don't talk that way." Then I told her what I had seen.

But I was worried, because I didn't understand what J. meant by telling me to stay in the yard, etc. I prayed to God to show me what she meant. What she meant according to the spirit was that I am hidden and buried in Christ Jesus, and the world can't find me because the things of the spiritual are hidden from all save them that be born of the spirit. God made her come to tell me to hold fast to my faith, because they all complained about me being so hard and uncompromising. Sometimes I got weak and wondered if I was right, and this was to show me that God was well pleased with me, and that I must hold fast to what I have. So let the world say what it will or may, if people around me don't live right I am going to tell them so, thus sayeth my God.

During the war we moved down on Front Street, in front of the old gashouse. My sister J. died in that old house, and my father took her in an old army wagon and buried her. The house we lived in was a big brick one, and we lived in the second floor. I don't know how many families lived there. We were all crowded in there together, both white and black.

After the war, or just before it was over, we moved to Franklin. Old man B. sent a wagon in to move us out there. We moved right back into the same log house we had used before the war started.

I went to work in the house. I don't know how much they paid Mama for my work, but I worked mighty hard rubbing candlesticks, molding candles, cleaning the house, and waiting on the table. I worked like a dog. Everybody was mistress and marster, even the little children. They were awfully fine and swell and did everything but say their prayers. On Sunday they usually sat around planning and plotting some devilment and meanness for us.

Around the cabin, the mothers usually spent the time combing the children's heads. They used cotton cords, and you could see head lice falling like gravel. We had meeting on certain Sundays, and we children had to sit on the platform. There was always some white people around. They just came to hear what was said and see what we were thinking about.

I used to get sick a lot. Mama would doctor on me with tea and grease made from weeds and marrow from bones. Children were more healthy then than they are now. I don't know why, but they were.

About four o'clock in the morning they would ring the bell for us to get up. I got up with my mother, dressed myself, got my buckets, and started to bringing water. This water was used for the house. From the time I got up until bedtime I didn't have no time to eat idle bread. I had some hard times. To stop to look at a book or anything else was almost death. I was beaten so much that I don't see how I kept my right senses.

On the farm adjoining ours was another plantation, and from what I saw old man F. do to the slaves, I think I was blessed to be treated no worse than I was. He had a lot of slaves, and he was a devil on earth. I never saw as many dead babies in my life as I did on his farm. He used to walk or ride down through the field and take his foot and kick poor women that were with child and cause them to have miscarriage right there in the field. Then he would call the Negro foreman to bring a cart and haul away this damn _____.

Women with small babies were allowed to take their babies to the field and put them under trees until nursing time. A woman had better not stop to suckle her baby until she was told to do it, else she would be beat almost to death. I actually saw old man F. walk through the field and, seeing a baby crying, take his stick and knock its brains out and call for the foreman to come and haul off the nasty, black rat.

Yes, in them days it was hell without fires. This is one reason why I believe in a hell. I don't believe a just God is going to take no such man as that into his kingdom.

One day some of us children were sitting on the adjoining fence looking over in the field at the slaves working. Old man F. came over to the fence and said, "Get down off of that fence, you black, nappy-headed bitches." Mistress heard him, and she came out and told him he was another son of a bitch, and that he was a damned liar and had better not touch one of her Negroes. They were cousins, but she cursed him out and told him she would kill him.

Them were some awful times. Many of the slaves were taught to steal from neighboring plantations. They would slip out at night and steal a cow or hog or corn and bring it home and lock it up in the smokehouse. They would steal in order to make their own provisions hold out. If a neighbor came to inquire about anything missing, the master would deny any knowledge of it. "No, I don't think any of my Negroes did it." They would say this, knowing all the time that the meat or corn was locked up in the smokehouse. Now these white folks are always talking about the Negro stealing. If they steal, it is mostly because they were taught to do it in slavery times. Not only stealing, but a lot of other devilment. Look at old N. that lived on the other side of us. He forced nearly every decent-looking slave woman he had. Williamson County is full of half-white children he got by his slaves. I used to hear my mistress talk about him a lot, but I had better not be caught listening. I heard just the same though, but I didn't have to hear. I had eyes I could see with, and I knowed there wasn't no white slaves over there. I saw and heard, too, a lot more than they thought I did.

My mother used to teach me how to listen and hear and keep my mouth shut. Sometimes she would have a little meeting, and some of the slaves from neighboring farms would come over. We children had better get out, or at least make like we were not listening to what was being said and done. She used to call me to her and say, "Now don't you tell anybody that so and so was here, or that you saw me do so and so." She would caution me, because she knew the white folks would be trying to pick some things out of me. Often they would get me up in the big house and ask me, "Wasn't so and so over in your mamma's cabin such and such a time, or didn't you see or hear them talking and planning to do this thing or that?" To all of this, I would either answer "I don't know" or "No." At the same time I would be trembling so that I could hardly speak, because I knew if they caught me in a lie I would get a whipping, and if I told, my mother would whip me. I was just in a hell all the time. But God has led me out of it and enabled me to reap some of the blessings of his goodness. I haven't got anything, but he comforts and keeps me.

I see many things now in the spirit. God shows me these things to let me know that he is well pleased with me.

Not long ago—about a year after J. died—I had a vision. It seemed to me that I was standing at a railroad station, and while I was standing there my eyes were fixed in one direction. I saw J. standing at the corner of a house, waving her apron. I never did look in her direction, but I could see her and hear her speak. As I stood there, I saw a train come out of the west. It was loaded with people, red-eyed, wild, and excited, and such scrambling and cutting up I never saw. I looked at it, and it went on by. I heard J. call and say, "Miss E., Mama did not get on that train." I hadn't seen E., my daughter, nor did I know she was there, but I heard her voice from the inside of the house. She said, "No, that wasn't Mama's train." I just stood there looking. I don't know what I was looking at or waiting for, but after a while I saw a pretty white train coming like lightning. I looked and saw myself on the train. I don't know how I got on, but when that train passed through, I was on it. The last thing I remember hearing was J. calling to E. and saying, "Mama got on that train," and E. said, "Uh huh."

I believe that God showed me this thing because everybody around here has been after me about saying that J. was lost.

hinder me not, ye much-loved sins

God first spoke to me when I was a boy twelve or thirteen years old. I remember it as well as if it happened yesterday. I was on Winstead's Hill, driving to town in a buggy. A voice spoke to me and said, "You must die and can't live." The thing scared me, and I looked about to see who spoke. About this time I heard singing. It was coming out of the east part of the world. I had never heard the words before, nor have I heard them since, but I remember them. It sounded like a multitude singing, and these are the words:

> In all my Lord's appointed ways,
> My journey I'll pursue.
> Hinder me not, ye much-loved sins,
> For I must not go with you!

It was some years after this before I had my soul delivered from hell, my blinded eyes opened, and my stammering tongue cut loose. But since that time I have rejoiced in the Lord, and I can talk about him in the darkest hours of midnight. There is no guess about it, for I know when I died and that I died to live again. When God delivered my soul from hell, it looked like I was going to be cast into that furnace and lost. But quicker than a flash he snatched my soul from the sea of doubt and the jaws of hell and carried me on to glory. He spoke to me and said, "Follow me, for I am the way, the truth, and the life. No man cometh to my father except through me." I went on to heaven and saw myself a sheep in a green pasture.

waist-deep in death

The Lord started me out when I was eight years old. We tried to seek the Lord. I went out on a Saturday evening behind an old stump, and old Satan, in my slumbers, ran me all around the stump that night.

I kept praying till I heard a voice. A voice told me, "I've chosen you before the dust of the earth." It told me, "I am God Almighty." A little, small child came to me on a motorcycle. The path we were traveling was no bigger than my little finger, but my foot just fitted it, and I followed this little white boy on the motorcycle to a little white building and a lot of little white children, all the same size, and all looking the same. I was in the midst of them, and then I heard a voice, "If I call you through deep water, it won't cover you; if I call you through fire, come on."

At eleven o'clock on Wednesday I heard a voice saying, "Many a snare shall touch your feet, but none shall get you." Then God took me off. I experienced death, the way I'm going to die. I was flying in the air. He throwed me down stiff. I was standing up ironing one morning, and I felt death creeping up on my toes, then to my knees, and finally I was waist-deep in death. Then I lost my sight, and God throwed me on the bed. I saw a stream of water. I saw my pastor, Willie Wilson. The Lord commanded me to go eight miles the other side of Franklin.

My fingers were like candlesticks. The next morning everything was white. My hands were like snow. They just shined. They looked like the sun was on them. Then God placed eyes all around my head. I died in hell, and the Boss man carried me to green pastures. I heard groanings while in hell. I saw dumpcarts dumping bodies. I heard the screaming and noise. Then he led me into the green pastures. I never heard such preaching in my life.

sitting
on cattles
of one
thousand hoofs

When the Lord freed my soul I was sitting out praying, and he told me that the sun was going down and said, "This day you got to die." And I said, "If I die I want to go with a prayer in my mouth." And while I was trusting him he carried me away in the spirit. He told me he was God, and there is none before him nor behind him. I saw the weeping willow trees and the sheep, and they all bowed at me.

When I died, I died at hell's dark door. I looked around me, and I saw a ladder let down from the top of a house. He told me I'd have to rise and follow him. I rose and stepped on the ladder and didn't stop till I reached the top. He told me he was my Father and I was his child. "Go and go in my name," he said.

One night I was sitting on cattles of one thousand hoofs. He told me to look and behold, because he was God.

He carried me to the third heaven year before last, and I shouted that place over, and I saw angels flying from place to place.

In the first heaven I seen people who'd been there for years and years. I saw my mother, sister, and brother, sitting as far back as possible.

I saw angels in the second heaven and the Lord spoke to me. He told me, "I am God the Messiah, I am God Almighty. There is none before me nor behind me. I made everything on this green earth. I even made the serpents, even the worms and birds." If he wanted water he wouldn't ask me for it, because he was God and made everything.

I was standing looking at him with my hands folded in front of me. When I was converted I seen myself in two parts. I was converted at home. I was converted twenty-four years this September. I wasn't at the church or mourner's bench.

I seen myself in the spirit; I seen one of my spirits washing the feet of the other spirit.

I don't wear my hair parted any other way but in the middle. I seen Christ with his hair parted in the center. He was white as snow. He had on a robe and girdle. I seen him in the spirit.